Gina Rushton is a journalist. Her reporting has appeared in *Australian Associated Press*, *BuzzFeed News*, *The Guardian*, *The Australian*, *The Saturday Paper*, *The Monthly*, *Crikey*, *Business Insider Australia* and *The West Australian*.

The Most Important Job in the World

GINA RUSHTON

MACMILLAN
Pan Macmillan Australia

First published 2022 in Macmillan by Pan Macmillan Australia Pty Ltd
1 Market Street, Sydney, New South Wales, Australia, 2000

A catalogue record for this book is available from the National Library of Australia

Typeset in 12.5/17.5pt Adobe Garamond Pro by Midland Typesetters, Australia
Printed by IVE

Quotes on pages 264–66 and 279 from Laurie Ann Paul reproduced by permission of the author and Oxford University Press.
Quotes on pages 101–102 from Kristin Dombek, *The Selfishness of Others: An Essay on the Fear of Narcissism*, Farrar, Straus and Giroux, 2016, reproduced with kind permission from the publisher.

For my mum, Cathy.

Contents

Author's note

The people in this book were either self-selecting or approached as experts. Some of their names have been changed for privacy reasons.

Not all people with uteruses are mothers and not all mothers have uteruses. The words woman and mother are used throughout this book, particularly where people identified as such, alongside more inclusive terms like parent or pregnant person.

Introduction

The question arrived as a sudden and unbearable cramp.

In January 2019, I found myself curled up in my boyfriend's bathroom, clawing at the tiles. I wanted to take a taxi to the hospital but the heavy pain in my abdomen had fastened me to the floor, so he called an ambulance. An internal ultrasound revealed I was bleeding out of my uterus and into my pelvic cavity. I needed emergency surgery. I was handed a piece of paper to sign, giving the surgeon permission to remove an ovary and to show I was aware they could puncture other organs on the way in. The doctor told me my left ovary was 'dead' after twisting and cutting off its own blood supply. I would go into surgery immediately because if the dead tissue was left inside of me, it could cause blood poisoning. This operation would affect my fertility, but we could discuss that once it was out.

You don't have to write about reproductive health for a living to know that halving the number of sites from which an egg can be produced might impact your ability to conceive. The doctor left, drawing the curtain behind her. I turned away from my boyfriend, wanting to privately assess the feeling rising inside of me. I was humiliated by the tears spilling onto the white hospital gown, betraying a secret vacillation, a pathetic flinching in the face of an operation that shouldn't faze a woman who had decided a decade earlier that she didn't want to be a mother.

'I don't want kids, you know I don't want kids,' I told him. I didn't know why I was so upset, I explained. 'It is probably just the morphine,' I offered. I called my mum just before the operation and repeated, 'I don't want kids, you know I don't want kids.'

'I know,' she said, an unfamiliar softness in her voice that I thought about afterwards.

In my mission to reject the most rudimentary of patriarchal mythology – that if you have the physical potential for motherhood, it should, as Adrienne Rich scoffs, be your 'single destiny and justification in life' – I had internalised an unfortunate tendency of the kind of feminism I was raised on. I became a woman with a preference, in this case not to be a parent, which was meant to be purely and unequivocally empowering simply because it was mine. In fact, I felt small and disoriented. In the end, a surgeon found that a large cyst had burst on my ovary, but it was alive. They did however find endometriosis, a condition in which tissue similar to the lining of the uterus grows beyond it. It can and likely will impact my fertility. Just as I thought

I might need longer to choose, I am accepting I might have even less time than the average woman approaching thirty. I am reckoning with the cost of ambivalence, the calculus involved when your wish for something, anything – a life centred on work, the possibility of a family, an abstraction of community – comes only in flashes and there is no hunger that lasts long enough to try satiating it.

I don't have loud enough answers for the questions I have barely whispered. My longstanding internal retort has been dismissive, uncoupled from any strong desire and defensively vague – *even if I was made of mother material, I would not volunteer for a position so chronically devalued and besides, the planet is dying of heat stroke.* This sweeping verdict that the world is no place for another child and that I am not supposed to be a parent at least needs an appendix if it is to be my final adjudication. The diagnosis has turned a sand timer inside of me. I am at the page to decide whether I want to have children. I am here to investigate and interview. I am here to read, to reflect and to write. I have given myself a deadline more specific than that my body will, because I am a journalist and that is the only way I get anything done.

Nine months.

At night I can hear the freight trains hiss and clatter past, 20 metres from my bedroom. My great-great-grandmother and namesake, Letitia, would have heard the trains scrape along the same line from her shack next to the tracks two stops east. She had ten children, eight who survived. For long stretches of time, she was alone with them while her husband was away moving livestock from place to place in the country. To survive, she worked as a wet nurse, breast-feeding richer women's children.

'How did she feed her own children then?' I ask my mother.

'She just had to hope there was enough milk left.'

From all accounts she loved motherhood as she did her children, but her options were not as mine are now. The control she had over the number and frequency of kids she was having was almost non-existent. It barely mattered how little time, how little support, how little money, how little milk she had for another human ten times over. A century later, I don't have to choose motherhood at all.

One more stop east on the train line is the house in which my mother lived married with three children by the age of 23, and four by 34 when I was born. My parents were growing a family at a time when houses in our city cost around six times the average full-time income, not almost 13 as they do now, when there wasn't a widespread fear about how the climate crisis will impact the next generation, when fertility was rarely assisted and when gender roles were if not set in stone, then a rigid default. My mother's decision to swap studying psychology and journalism for teaching, a more family-friendly profession, while my father pursued law, would be a different, longer conversation for me and my partner now, almost five decades later. I have choices my great-great-grandmother never did and more time than my mother had to make them. This is not to patronise the women whose blood runs through mine but to acknowledge that while my body, my hopes and my desires are still valued less than those of men, I have more agency than I would have in years past. I have options, even if I'm learning they each have an expiry date.

The question of who owns a body and who can intervene in its fate has consumed most of my working life so far. Every day for several years I reported on reproductive choice, which is to say I documented power and control. I interviewed woman after woman about the ways social stigma, inequality, the law, and the state had each obstructed their access to contraception and abortion. Few people have been so professionally occupied with the risks of coercing people into parenthood. Even fewer have written hundreds of news articles about how compromised and conditional bodily autonomy can be. I know it has left me carrying an unreasonable need to prove to myself that this is a decision I am making without intervention. That this is my body, that this is my choice. I might come to the page with a singular paranoia, but I am also just another person, unsure of herself and her future, trying to make a decision.

Nothing so quickly confirms what you love and fear most about the world and yourself like the question of whether or not you want children. My friendships with women who are perpetually loving, blossoming, failing, forgiving, growing, reaching towards a better world with a grace that should never have been demanded of them. The kids, marching with their signs. The fathers in my life softening, the mothers taking space. My partner, gently challenging expectations of what a relationship with a man could be. My elderly neighbour leaving a single homegrown tomato on my doorstep in the middle of a pandemic. My unstoppable niece, half-naked, zooming on her scooter down a hill through a public park, refusing to heed or wear a shirt, speeding with the confidence and fearlessness of a middle-aged man, somehow yet to realise girls must be obliging, sweet and modest. My hubristic belief in my own ability to take good care of others. The bluebells I sold to my mother's friend as bulbs when I was a child still blooming each September two decades later. Notions of a home, stable in the way mine wasn't.

The graphs showing emissions and inequities, lines inching towards the top right corner of each square. The sense that everyone is hardening, digging their heels into dogmatism. The struggle to think of a single friend in a relationship with a man where there is a fair division of any kind of labour. The 200-and-something weeks of exposure to readers who believe women are overreacting, women are asking for it, women are incubators. Tracing the identities of one of my trolls and discovering he was a boy, not yet a man. The days where I hear a whisper in the wind: *I'm broken and can't be repaired*. Fires blazing along the Arctic Circle. Loving someone who is in addiction for a long time and learning how neither love nor time always heals. Every parliamentary debate I've reported on in which physical sovereignty was debated by men who fetishised motherhood, *the most important job in the world*, while supporting policies that made life harder for mothers.

There are no deciding factors, only feelings.

I am a member of a generation that often feels impotent in the face of endless uncertainty. The question of children thrusts us into a time beyond now, demanding we come up with more than whatever gets us through the present while the only assurance we've had about what lies ahead is that it will be worse.

I begin these nine months of thinking, writing, deciding in the early stages of a global pandemic, unfolding alongside a climate crisis. It feels especially foolish to want something specific from the coming years. How do we let ourselves imagine any future without being overpowered by despair or manipulated by hope? I am trying not to self-soothe in the ways millennials know best. I am trying not to reflexively temper my faith in the future with irony and fatalism. I am trying not to whip myself into a delusional frenzy so my despondency can't be heard over the hum of a mantra: if I work hard enough, grow enough, control my surroundings enough, believe enough, march enough, consume ethically enough, read enough, I will cool the planet and subdue behemoth institutions or insidious cultural forces that are completely beyond one person's control. Recycling and sharing memes in the group chat about global collapse won't sustain me into my 30s, with or without children.

I want to map the differences between giving up and, as Pablo Servigne and Raphaël Stevens write, accepting 'the death of a future that was dear to us, a future that was reassuring, however irrational it might have been'. At a time when the planet is warming and people are wondering how many, if any, children they should be having, I want to understand how much power and responsibility individuals have when it comes to family planning. I begin these nine months as eight teenagers, supported by an 86-year-old Catholic nun, take on the federal government in court to stop the extension of a coal mine in my state. They invoke the environment minister's duty of care to protect young people against climate change. What do we owe to our children who will fall heir to a planet different from the one we grew up in? What do we owe to the planet when it comes to adding another human to it? What do we owe to our own hopes and dreams when governments are allowing businesses to emit carbon with impunity? The environment minister will ultimately approve the coal mine despite the government's unresolved appeal against the class action. It will extract 168 million tonnes of coal over the next 25 years.

I want to know how people parent without living in permanent denial or perpetual dread. I will find people who are watching species die, authoring papers on rising sea levels, studying renewable energy and protecting their children's lungs from bushfire smoke to ask them where they put their hope and fear.

The Most Important Job in the World

In Sophie Mackintosh's dystopian novel *Blue Ticket*, on the day of your first period you enter a lottery and you're handed either a white ticket, designating you as a person who will have to bear children, or a blue ticket, the coveted option, which grants you a compulsory contraceptive insertion and a childless future. Inevitably, some blue ticketholders wrench the devices from their uteruses and conceive and some white ticketholders try to abort their forced pregnancies. 'Having a child is both the most rational and irrational decision possible, in this world,' says Marisol, a blue ticketholder who is on the run from the authoritarian regime under which her pregnancy isn't allowed. 'This fucking awful, beautiful world, which I can't stop loving, though I have considered it, I have evaluated and counted the ways.'

To have a child feels like a leap of faith in myself as I am and this awful, beautiful world as it will be, or an act of faith in our ability as parents and children to survive transience. I find in myself and in others a fear about what children will inherit not just in the earth in which we plant them in but in their roots; a contemporary consciousness of how harm moves through generations. When I was a child, to be inconspicuous was a virtue and it seemed parents were also less inspected. But now even hypothetical children feel visible to us and we feel visible to them with all our flaws in a way that feels new. My mother had a single ultrasound across four pregnancies. It feels as though we now scan ourselves for complications before we even know if we want to be parents. The question of whether or not to have children forces us to think deeply about our own impermanence while reminding us that we might be here just long enough to pass along what we love and fear. I will seek out people who are scared about what their legacy might be when it comes to their genetics, their cultural mores, their trauma and their tendencies, and thinkers who could help me answer how much agency we have over this. Is an awareness of how you were raised and how you want to raise your children enough? How much are we trying to prevent harm and how much are we trying to control outcomes? What if all our kids actually absorbed was the millennial hyper-cognisance of consequences and we raise a generation of risk-averse neurotics?

For women in relationships with men, the question of motherhood intensifies many of the lessons we are unlearning about our place in our own partnerships. In considering whether to make an irreversible decision to have a child, we are often considering an investment in the longevity of dynamics we have spent years questioning. We still hear echoes of the messages we were told as children about how boys and girls should or should never express our needs and what we are allowed to ask of each other. The childfree women I know have already tasted motherhood. We have given unconditional love, care, domestic and emotional work to those around us, including partners.

I am not the first dutiful daughter to resist the spectre of maternal responsibility. The year I was born, *Men Are from Mars, Women Are from Venus* was published. The self-help bestseller answered the frustrations of heterosexual relationships, where gender was seen as the inherent cause of friction. In this book, the highest ranked work of nonfiction in the 1990s, women were encouraged to straddle a planetary divide by cajoling men into doing stuff they apparently weren't biologically wired for, like willingly contributing emotionally and domestically to a home and relationship. In its gender essentialism, the book assured readers the origin of their relationship problems was inevitable and in doing so, 'renormalised heterosexual misery for a new generation', as Jane Ward writes.

I want jokes in which women are mothers to childish men to be incomprehensibly boring to my niece and nephew by the time they are in romantic relationships. At a time when heterosexuality has become the easiest convention to satirise, how do we take relationships with men seriously? I don't want to start a family drenched in this pessimism, or worse, breathless with gratitude that my partner does as much as me. How do we test assumptions and expectations around love and labour, regardless of our gender and sexuality? How do we find symmetry in care and in communication that feels sustainable enough to hold a third human? How do we do so without expending more of the work we are weary from? At a time when we are often asking one person to give us, as Esther Perel says, 'what an entire village used to provide', I want to name what we should expect from our partners and what we have failed to build in our other relationships, including in the one we have with ourselves.

I begin these nine months at a time when we need to social distance and sanitise. Each day we are reminded of our connectedness, our ability to keep each other safe and how we have always breathed in the strangers we ignored. People are leaving toilet paper, cans of lentils and loaves of bread for each other at the end of my street. I am surprised, then sad that I am surprised. I want to understand why I can't imagine building a community strong enough to support me into my old age without family. What does kin mean to someone born just before a divorce in a family that fractured in every direction? I want to understand why I imagine modern motherhood as inherently isolating, detached from community, when I was frequently minded by neighbours and friends of my mother and she would mind their children too. I want to find my way back to a proximity with other humans beyond the nuclear family, with or without my own children.

Revisiting my decision to reject motherhood will mean reconsidering what the word means. Why would anyone become a mother? Not a woman with a child but a mother, as I was first led to believe she should be – infinitely nourishing, serene, sweet, soft, without anger, without needs, without self and later, as she was revised, with a meaningful career. Deborah Levy writes that mother is the woman the whole world has 'imagined to death' and still here I am, needing to revive and reimagine her again until the

12

last unsavoury archetypes I am holding on to crumble in my hands. I need to know precisely what I am saying no to. I need to acknowledge how witnessing my mother cook, clean and care for four children who had different needs for their security and sanity has defined the word for me.

I need to examine everything I have learned about how rewarding a career is and how thankless parenthood would be. I am wary of romanticising the unpaid work of motherhood. I have watched too many politicians prove that you can idealise something without valuing it. I have live-blogged their comments in parliamentary debates, I have fact-checked their claims. You can dehumanise someone by putting them on a pedestal because saints don't have needs. They don't need paid parental leave, they don't need affordable childcare or housing, they don't need freedom from punitive welfare programs and they definitely don't need safe, affordable and legal access to choose whether they continue a pregnancy. I don't want to be thanked once a year in May because I am need-less. I don't want to enter into something laden with guilt and judgement. The sentimentalisation of motherhood as the God-given purpose of all women with uteruses lingers even though our parents' generation began to resist parenthood as the default. People my age are still pushing against this while simultaneously questioning what came in its wake: the ascendance of paid work as the primary place of self-fulfilment.

Revisiting my decision to reject motherhood will mean reconsidering whether a career is what I want to prioritise instead. The feminism I grew up with was anti-maternal or at least calling for women to become 'more' than 'just' mothers. Meaning-making happened outside the home. In parenthood we are expected to accept that labouring for love requires no compensation, in the modern workplace we are expected to accept that any love we have for our labour is worth so much it can even supplement cash in a pay cheque. If the expectation is now to love what you do in parenthood and find a career that allows you to do what you love, I want to understand the fine print.

Revisiting my decision to reject motherhood will mean reconsidering what lives I might live if I move beyond defining myself through any form of labour. I want to fantasise about the space between the myths of woman as womb and woman as worker to consider a life in which my purpose is tied to neither. I want to consider a life in which my identity is not contingent on the labour my body produces in reproduction or production. A libido for other kinds of creation.

A friend who is nearing 30 calls and talks about a change she can feel inside herself. It is not whatever smug biological-clock watchers think happens when you reach this age. It is something else. She doesn't want children. She likes her job but has realised it will never be everything to her. She wants to travel but can't because of the pandemic. The mess of her early 20s is over. The parade of men we knew never deserved her but who nonetheless taught her more about herself, the stress of study, the years of late nights partying then the years of late nights working, the travelling, the learning and unlearning, the knowledge of who she might be and what she might want. 'I've done the work, I feel ready for something,' she says. She is describing a richness within herself, an absence of toxicity, a readiness, an ability to sustain growth; a fertility. She is wondering where to plant her roots. She is ready to unfurl.

I am one woman, a lucky one, with a big set of liberties and a smaller set of burdens influencing my decision. I have had the immeasurable freedom of time to consider this question in the abstract, which is not afforded to many people considering how and with whom to build a family, biologically or otherwise. I want to look beyond the doubts I have about myself and my own place in the workplace, in a relationship with a man, in a body that might be infertile, in a dynasty of dysfunction, in a country where colour is draining from the coral and smoke will more frequently fill the sky. I don't want to draw myself into my own windowless hesitation, where I can't see storms nor appreciate how sheltered I am from them. What are the stakes for a middle-class white woman considering middle-class white motherhood? I have spent years immersed in various battles for reproductive rights that have been organised around women like me – those who want to prevent pregnancy. I am learning. I am expanding my concept of reproductive oppression to include everyone with a uterus who is obstructed not only from preventing or ending pregnancy but from continuing them safely, free from violence and discrimination. How have my safe interactions with medical and legal institutions blinkered my understanding of how other women experience them? Not one of the challenges posed by potential parenthood are borne evenly by everyone and they are rarely heaviest for white, cis-gendered, able-bodied women who are in relationships with men. I am hoping that the experiences of others will speak where I cannot and should not.

'Whether I want kids is a secret I keep from myself – it is the greatest secret I keep from myself,' Sheila Heti writes in *Motherhood*, a novel in which the protagonist tries to answer the same question I am. I begin these nine months feeling disconnected from myself and what I want from the rest of my life, unpractised at accessing my own wanting without self-censoring. My friends and I, all in our late 20s, bought Heti's book a few years ago believing that we would finish it knowing one way or the other if we were going to be parents. I suspect some of my friends wanted a book that would reassure them that to have a child wasn't to fail at feminism, ruin a career, forfeit creative fulfilment, risk a relationship, or refuse action on climate change. I was foolishly hoping it would convince me of the opposite – I wanted an object that I could press into the hands of my loved ones to explain my decision not to have kids. Instead, we were left with more questions.

When I was a child, I was desperate to believe in God like my mother did. I wanted to bypass goodness, accountability, community, and anything else that might remediate the things that kept me up at night. I wanted a set of commands I could claim as morals. Now that I know how arbitrary and harmful these rules can be, now that I know you can't manufacture faith, now that I'm older, I just want a conviction that feels enduring enough to confront fear as I feel it. Inspired by the ancient Chinese divination text *I Ching*, Heti's main character creates her own kind of clairvoyance, posing yes–no questions while tossing three coins which give her answers. I am not just aiming to answer yes or no; I am also trying to legitimise the questions we are striving to answer and identify those that have been thrust upon us and from which we could liberate ourselves. I'm here to find priorities I can live with, love even, in the time it takes to grow a baby.

In a letter to his brothers in 1817, poet John Keats used the term 'negative capability' to describe 'being in uncertainties, mysteries, doubts, without any irritable reaching after fact and reason'. I am trying to get more comfortable with the questions, curious not craving, calm about what I don't know. I want to get better at living in the in-between despite knowing I might have limited time to ask whether I *should* have children before I can ask whether I even can. Endometrial-like cells will continue to grow beyond my uterus regardless of what I choose. It's possible to feel indignant about the speed at which we need to consider these questions if we are to leave enough time for kids, should we want them, but I can't help but feel blessed by the urgency.

How lucky we are, as women, to be conscripted by our own fertility into asking these huge philosophical questions in our 20s and fighting for what we want from our future. It need not be an unresolvable burden but an opportunity to ask not just what we want from our own lives but what kind of world we want to move towards whether we parent or not.

Gestation is depicted as a peaceful process but in fact it is biological paradox, a bloody war mediated by the placenta which protects the embryo from being immuno-logically attacked like any other foreign matter would. In pregnancy, you don't just grow a foetus but a whole new guardian organ that gathers food and defends your baby from the body's own desires and defences. At first the placenta distracts the body from this piece of non-self and then fights the uterus for blood to nourish the growing embryo. The parent within the parent before there is a child. I have never allowed space to grow the idea of myself as a mother and now, on the page, I will find the parent within so I can see the person I am renouncing. Nine months for hypotheticals, nine months for honesty. Nine months to call mothers, fathers, people who do not want children, experts, and friends. Nine months to weave something through which I can filter hope and fear, mine and that I find in each conversation.

I always believed the answer would come before the question, as we're led to believe it does. The desire for children would just appear, unbidden and then unwavering.

I never heard that 'yes' and so I assumed it was a 'no'. Instead, the question came first and fast, uncomfortable, and unanswered. I can't build a life around a preference; I need to make a choice.

1

Reproductive rights

The right to use your body to bear children. The right not to. The right to make informed decisions about this, free from judgement, coercion or deception. The people I interviewed were often incredulous that these rights were compromised or on the precipice of revocation. *I had no idea it was still a crime. I had no idea I would have to borrow money. I had no idea a doctor could refuse to help me. I had no idea a doctor would lie to me. I had no idea I could be harassed outside a clinic. I had no idea I would have to travel interstate. I had no idea I couldn't get it in the public system. I had no idea a hospital could turn me away if there was a complication. I had no idea I'd have to go into an induced labour on a maternity ward while hearing other babies crying and knowing I would not leave with ours.* Their agency was more conditional than they knew. Journalists are just vessels through which stories travel but we fool ourselves into thinking they don't change us in transit. Sometimes I think these interviews have left me shadowboxing, convinced I will not have the final say over how I use my body.

'There are a thousand different reasons why people go down that path and it is nobody's business why,' Annie told me. Not long before I went into hospital, I interviewed the mother of two who had been pregnant as the result of a rape. Annie was at eight weeks gestation, early enough for a medical abortion, but she booked in for a surgical termination because she did not want to cramp and expel the evidence of her trauma. Even if she had resources to raise a third child, she 'didn't want to explain to this kid where they came from'.

This was before her state of Queensland had safe-access zones protecting patients from picketers. I had already reported on the clinic Annie attended because footage had been taken of protesters trying to hand a plastic foetal doll to another patient. 'This is a little 12-week-old baby,' the woman in the video says, following the patient towards the door. 'That little one that you have has a heartbeat, ten fingers, ten toes and God hates the hands that shed his blood.' The patient can be heard begging them to leave her alone.

When Annie and her father approached the same clinic, one picketer blocked her path and another touched her arm. 'I just kept my eyes on the door or on the floor,' she told me. 'I felt embarrassed. I felt ashamed. People were grabbing me.' I didn't include the last bit of our interview in the story, but it followed me into the emergency ward.

Annie told me that since her abortion, she'd had several miscarriages, all for planned pregnancies. She admitted sheepishly that she felt like this was 'karma' even though she felt certain that her abortion was the right decision. I told her it wasn't the first nor would it be the last time a woman I interviewed would explain to me this tension between a decision they felt was hard but right. We talked about how stigma can live on inside someone. I thought about how I knew the condemnation of each story I published would come before it arrived on my screen. The words did not disappear even after I emptied the trash folder.

Access to abortion was not something I gave any thought to before 2016. I could only name a few women I knew who had accessed what I assumed was a seldom chosen but attainable procedure. It wasn't until learning that it was in fact incredibly common – one in six Australian women in their 30s have had an abortion – but rarely accessible that my editor and I found ourselves confronting a situation so undocumented that it would generate stories for the next four years. By 2020 I had likely spoken to more people in Australia about their abortions than anyone else in the country, sans medical professionals or counsellors. The patchwork of legality, the fragile network of doctors who had to become advocates, the travel, the prohibitive cost. Unfolding across the hundreds of articles I wrote were different versions of the same truth – in this country, reproductive choice expands and contracts according to the resources you have, the means to afford travel, accommodation, privacy, lost days of income, childcare and the procedure. Unlike other common medical procedures, there is no widespread public access to abortion and people often need to find money at short notice to go to a private clinic. When I began reporting on the issue, a woman in one state down south could access a surgical termination at no cost at a public hospital while those in another state up north were paying private clinics $800 for two pills that were supposed to cost $38. Notorious 'conscientious objectors', sometimes the only doctor for kilometres, judged and obstructed with impunity. Cash-strapped women's organisations fundraised on Facebook to cover the cost of abortion for people without housing or those experiencing violence. Abortion was decriminalised in four jurisdictions in as many years but in failing to make healthcare affordable or available, governments forced patients to rely on good luck or good will to access the procedure.

Women, with or without uteruses, already know their bodies can be treated as public property. Week by week I learned how many people can and will intervene in the choices women make about our own bodies and our own futures. Once you understand the body as public property you begin to see how the state can also degrade what it owns through neglect.

After a couple of articles, a handful of people I knew messaged to tell me about their abortions. Within months, it was dozens. I found girls I had gone to high school with, journalists in other states, mothers and grandmothers who had had backyard abortions, all wanting to tell someone, often for the first time. Halfway through dinner, a friend took a sip of wine, closed her eyes and, keeping them shut, said, 'I know you won't judge me'. I moved the food out of the way, held her hand and waited. She turned her head to the right, looking past me, the tears on her left cheek catching the light, and only met my eye when she had finished her story. Over the next four years people would tell me again and again that no matter what, whether the law, their doctors, or their families helped or hindered them, they would have ended their pregnancy somehow, safely or unsafely. A woman approached me at a bookshop and told me about her great-grandmother, who had many children and found herself pregnant for the last time. She tried to end the pregnancy herself out of desperation and when it went wrong, was too scared to get help as abortion was a crime. This woman said her own grandmother watched the white bed sheets turn red as her mother slowly died. 'They kept changing the linen again and again. But it just kept getting soaked with blood. It was all they could do. *Change the linen, change the linen, change the linen.*'

In 2018, Senator Fraser Anning introduced a motion calling on the government to fund counselling for women who wanted to have abortions to inform them about the 'development of the unborn baby', alternatives such as adoption, and the risks of abortion. 'We have seen outrage over the destruction of kangaroos, yet where is the same compassion when it comes to an unborn human?' Anning, who later that year invoked a Nazi euphemism for genocide while arguing against Muslim migration, asked the chamber. The motion was redundant. All Australians accessing abortion services publicly or privately are offered counselling and informed of any risks, and there is also a free national counselling hotline for anything to do with conception, pregnancy, birthing, and postnatal care.

Anti-abortion politicians do this a lot. They pass meaningless motions or suggest unnecessary amendments to proposed legislation – a gestational limit that is already regulated by clinical guidelines, a caveat forbidding sex-selective abortions that would only work if doctors were mind-readers, an amendment creating a separate criminal offence for anyone who pressures someone into having an abortion as if intimidation isn't already a crime. Their claims so rarely matched the lived experiences of each person I interviewed, and the grandstanding was never about practicality – for that you'd need truth – but the message it sent. Behind the propositions I fact-checked remained a suspicion of women and their capacity to make choices of any virtue for themselves.

I have interviewed women who could not fund the cost of the termination let alone the cost of raising a child. One of the first stories I published was about research that showed women in Australia were delaying paying bills and forgoing food and groceries to cover the cost. There was the woman who said she paid for some of her abortion with 20 cent pieces from her friends' tip jars. The woman who told me she had lived on packet noodles for weeks afterwards. The woman who borrowed half and cashed in all of her accrued annual leave to cover the rest. All the pregnant people who relied on women's organisations to fundraise for them via Facebook statuses – a 14-year-old without accommodation who could not attend her local Catholic public hospital, a young homeless woman who was pregnant after being sexually assaulted while staying in a squat and had tried to induce a miscarriage with over-the-counter medications, a mother of three whose ex-partner had been jailed for the physical and sexual violence he had perpetrated against her.

I have interviewed mothers who told me that having another child would not be the right choice for the children they already had. A mother of four with a child who had a degenerative genetic condition who did not want her and her husband's energy to be divided again, the woman who did not want another child to be tied to a violent father, the woman who was barely coping with her existing children.

Jamie had been hospitalised for severe postpartum depression seven months after the birth of her son and started a relationship with her abuser a few months later. 'I was in a women's-only mental health housing and a vulnerable person with a young child,' she told me. Jamie's partner, who was eventually charged and jailed for assaulting her, refused to wear protection as it 'didn't feel as good'.

'He knew I would take risks if he didn't want to use protection because in this abusive dynamic, I would have done anything to make him happy,' she said. They had decided to terminate the pregnancy but she wanted a few days to accept and process the decision. 'He responded violently, assaulted me, stomped on my stomach and grabbed me by the throat.' Jamie said access to affordable abortion saved her life. 'I could never condemn myself, my son or that child to being tied to an abusive man for 18 years, giving him that hold on me, giving him any right to contact me ever again,' she said. 'I had to make that sacrifice to sever that tie.'

Laura had been a victim of domestic abuse after she fell pregnant and wanted an abortion. 'I was coerced into keeping the baby due to my partner's emotional abuse, controlling and harassing tactics, which later escalated into physical abuse,' she told me. 'The entire nine months, I was trapped in his control, reliant on him and subjected to emotional turmoil.' The violence does not stop with the pregnancy; in fact pregnancy can be a risk factor for violence. More than half (54 per cent) of women living with abusive partners experience violence during pregnancy, and pregnancy also significantly increases a woman's risk of being killed by her partner.

'I think domestic violence is about control and [during pregnancy] she is starting to focus on this new life, her body is changing, she is developing that natural maternal care for the baby,' Hannah Dahlen, professor of midwifery at Western Sydney University, told me. 'Men are starting to see their possession slip from their grip.'

The Most Important Job in the World

It can also tighten their grip. I sat waiting with Isabelle in a small room next to the court in which her ex-partner was about to be sentenced for her rape. Her leg shook nervously as she read over her victim impact statement, preparing herself. She had a congenital heart condition which meant she could not use the contraceptive pill when they were together and her pregnancies were high-risk. She had three children because her partner had refused to wear protection and she did not feel like she had any control over when they had sex. 'It felt like an obligation and another chore, and I just gave it to him so he'd shut up, because I didn't want the fighting,' she told me. She also had multiple abortions throughout their relationship, against his wishes. 'He wanted me to have babies because that meant staying home another five years.' Isabelle lost an enormous amount of blood in her final pregnancy because she also had placenta previa, a condition where the placenta lies low and may cover the cervix, blocking the baby's exit during birth. 'I nearly died.' She looked at her partner after the birth and thought, '*How dare you? And all because you wanted sex.*' A jury found him guilty of one count and not guilty of another count of rape. He was sentenced to four years imprisonment with a non-parole period of two years and nine months.

Kate, who had a medical abortion on the eve of Mother's Day a few years earlier, whispered down the phone line so as not to wake her sleeping baby. 'For me, the termination was an act of love for my other children and a reaffirmation

29

of my love for my relationship,' she said. 'If I hadn't had an abortion my life would be over . . . I know I would have taken my own life and left many children without a mum.' Other women did not think they could survive going off their medication for the duration of a pregnancy.

Most abortions happen in the first nine weeks of gestation. It was, for most people I spoke to, an instant decision to end a pregnancy even if doing so was complex or confronting. Liz, a Christian, was told at 11 weeks that her foetus had abnormalities. Her father told her if the Lord wanted her to keep the pregnancy, he would make that clear. She knew she wanted to terminate. 'Abortion is portrayed in Christianity as being this cold and callous money-making business, and that if you have an abortion you'll never really get rid of the guilt because you'll suffer for the rest of your life,' she said. 'I felt really peaceful about it.'

There were women who felt unadulterated relief about their decision and others who did not regret their abortions but who had a real sense of grief about them. Sadness, even regret, is not a medical condition but I have repeatedly debunked a widely discredited phenomenon, coined 'post-abortion syndrome' by an American anti-abortion campaigner in the 1980s, that suggests women who have terminated a pregnancy allegedly develop a condition in which they are more prone to suicidal ideation, alcohol and drug abuse among other things. The tragic consequence of this misinformation is the women I interviewed who were sad about their abortions felt there was no space in the pro-choice movement to acknowledge their feelings without giving power to religious charlatans. 'It has taken me a long time to let myself feel sad because I am so pro-choice – I felt like that meant you're not allowed to be ashamed and you're not allowed to be sad,' one woman told me. She was a lesbian who had fallen pregnant to a man on a cruise ship in a one-night stand while she was grieving her partner of ten years, who had recently died.

Another woman who had an abortion as a teenager said, 'Any sign of weakness is co-opted by a narrative that I don't want to contribute to because I'm not grieving for the child I could have had . . . Reducing it to a decision that you have to be 100 per cent comfortable with really erases the experience of people who – for whatever reason – need to terminate a pregnancy but who would, in other circumstances, have kept it. It doesn't leave room for people who have conflicted emotions about it.'

Just as I stopped writing about reproductive rights full-time, a landmark ten-year study was published that confirmed what I had always believed: not only that my interviewees' choices were painfully considered, as I could hear in their voices and through their tears, but that their self-knowledge could in fact be prescient. It wasn't an aimless prediction, a foolish clairvoyance, but an awareness of their own material conditions. Diana Greene Foster and her team of psychologists, epidemiologists, physicians, demographers, economists and public health researchers conducted and analysed almost eight thousand interviews of women who were either allowed or denied the abortion they wanted in the United States for *The Turnaway Study*. Some gave birth after they were denied an abortion because they had been just over a clinic's gestational limit and the rest were just under that limit and received an abortion. 'When asked why they want to end a pregnancy, women give specific and personal reasons,' Greene writes. 'And their fears are borne out in the experiences of women who carry unwanted pregnancies to term.' The data should not matter – agency should not only be afforded the prophetic – but it does matter because for decades women have been told they are making rushed, uninformed, selfish choices to end their pregnancies.

The Turnaway Study found women who were denied their abortions were more likely to live in poverty. It found that women who were unable to terminate their pregnancies were more likely to stay in contact with their violent partner. It found the children of women who had to carry an unwanted pregnancy to term scored worse on several measures of health and development than those whose mother was able to access the abortion she wanted. There were no differences in the women just over or just under the gestational limits when it came to baseline mental health, history of trauma or drug and alcohol use – they were similar to national estimates. Those who had been denied an abortion had slightly worse mental health in the short-term but within a year the two groups found themselves back at similar levels. These women proved resilient to the experience of giving birth following an unwanted pregnancy. Greene found no evidence that abortion hurt women and found that women who had terminated their pregnancy were more frequently better off – physically, financially, professionally – than those who were denied one. Two women who were denied their abortions died of childbirth-related causes.

The data does not say having a child makes your life worse. It says when women want to end a pregnancy, there are real repercussions to being denied that choice. It says that women know themselves and their families and use that knowledge to make choices. Women who were given their abortion were more likely to intentionally become pregnant in the next five years than women who were not.

The most successful narrative the anti-abortion lobby has authored, here and abroad, is to frame the decision to terminate a pregnancy as a decision to reject motherhood. A desperate teenager or a selfish hussy might terminate a pregnancy but a *mother,* she who has known what it is to give and sustain life, surely could not. This myth has proved powerful, affirming that women who have abortions are occupied with themselves only. They are not nurturing, they are not gentle, they are not maternal. The truth is that it is estimated that more than half of women in Australia who have abortions are mothers. The women in my stories were making decisions as mothers, even for the few who weren't already or would never become mothers. The idea that women do not have adequate information, intelligence or intuition to make decisions for themselves but somehow have the innate ability to care for a child often dovetails neatly with the idea that abortion is to reject mother-hood, either through selfishness, incomprehension that it is life growing inside of them – *here is an ultrasound* – or ignorance about how easy and fulfilling parenting can be.

Nowhere was this myth more ruthlessly mongered than in the debate about abortions after the first or second trimester. Each push to decriminalise abortion has been met with an aggressive misinformation campaign of letter-boxing, advertising and even robocalls – 'more babies will die if you vote Labor' – about what they termed 'partial-birth abortions' or 'abortion up to birth'. Examining these claims in parliamentary and public debate took up too much of my reporting. Then Senator for South Australia Cory Bernardi claimed later term abortions were when 'you've known you're pregnant for 34 or 35 weeks and you decide you're going to have a termination'. 'How can anyone justify the killing of a baby at that point?' he asked the chamber. 'It is murder of an unborn baby that could exist outside of the womb, and it shouldn't be done on what I would say is the simple demand, or the selfish demand, of an individual involved.' However, Bernardi's claim was erroneous as women can't just *decide* to have an abortion at 34 or 35 weeks.

As many doctors did, Queensland obstetrician and maternal-foetal medicine specialist Dr Carol Portmann explained that if anyone wanted a termination at 30 weeks 'they would just have to go on to have the baby'. Terminations beyond the utmost gestational limit – 22 or 24 weeks in most areas – can't be done on a patient's whim, they are only permitted after strenuous medical consultation, often with an ethics board.

Patients are often denied abortions past a certain gestation but those who are granted them are in devastating situations. 'It is mostly brain problems which weren't visible earlier on, and parents know their child will survive for a period of time with no quality of life, whether that is a matter of days or up to a year, and pass away, and parents feel they simply can't watch their child in suffering,' she said. 'These are conditions which are ultimately always lethal.' Portmann told me in her more than two decades clinical experience she had never been asked to perform a termination after 28 weeks for psychosocial reasons. 'It is always because a baby has [been] found to have such a severe heart or brain injury, or where the mother's life is at risk.'

Emily, a mother who terminated a wanted pregnancy at 19 weeks, told me about Maya. 'She was really sick and it was unlikely that she would survive to term, but if she did she may have been born dead, died in the process or lived a short and painful life for a few days where she wouldn't see life outside the hospital . . . It would have been cruel to force her to live through that pain.' Emily described the agony of the process in which her labour was induced, and the unforgettable thud of her dead foetus hitting the bedpan. 'Post-birth you have bleeding, which was almost reassuring that I had this connection to her,' she said. 'It

35

almost made something that was very surreal seem quite real because while it was a day, it was not just a day you get over: you're forever changed by it.'

Senator Barry O'Sullivan said, while moving a motion to condemn Queensland's (eventually successful) abortion decriminalisation, 'I can hardly hold the thought: a baby who is seconds off being named, or even pre-named in many cases – certainly, in my family line and in most of the families I'm involved with – will be euthanised.'

Melanie McKenzie, who runs a not-for-profit organisation to support women and their families who have received a poor or fatal diagnosis during pregnancy, testified at a Senate inquiry in support of decriminalising abortion in Queensland: 'These parents face perhaps the hardest decision of all when told of a fatal diagnosis of their unborn baby: whether or not to have a late termination,' she said. 'This is never a decision taken lightly or without much medical testing, diagnosis, and medical advice.' In 2010 McKenzie's fourth son, Harrison, lived for just 28 hours due to an incurable condition, a diaphragmatic hernia, diagnosed at 20 weeks gestation. 'We chose to continue with our pregnancy,' she said. 'I watched my son, who was in obvious pain, having to have invasive medical procedures.'

Senator Amanda Stoker said during Senator O'Sullivan's motion, 'How can we be investing the entire weight of the medical profession's expertise and of public expense in saving premature children in some circumstances while we simultaneously kill healthy children born in other circumstances?'

Abby, a mother who terminated a pregnancy at 24 weeks, told me she waited for four days in hospital in unbearable limbo while her case was reviewed by a Crown solicitor. She was told by doctors she needed to terminate as soon as possible as her foetus' heart was barely beating. 'I was terrified of having a dead body inside of me,' she told me. 'I was in labour for five hours and scared the entire time because, on top of the immense pain, I knew I was going to give birth to a dead baby.' The family had a private burial at a cemetery, where they visit every day to lay fresh flowers at his grave.

The next month Senator Janet Rice stood up, tears in her eyes, and said to her fellow senators in the chamber, 'Most . . . late-term abortions are because there are issues with the development of the foetus, and that was certainly the case for mine, and yet [other senators] are willing to stand here in this place and call me a murderer . . . Anybody who wants to look at the facts about late-term abortions will see that a woman having a late-term abortion has gone through a huge thought process, discussion, and consideration of whether it's the right thing to do.' Later, she told me, 'I know how much impact those words have, and my emotion showed in the Senate.'

I am no longer surprised about what people will blame on abortion. The Northern Territory politician who said the jurisdiction's diminishing share of goods and services tax profits was due to a slow in population growth because of abortion. The budget might be repaired if the government 'promoted' women continuing unwanted pregnancies.

During the bushfires, my local anti-abortion organisation told its members that the deadly blazes were ordered by God for our own good and would continue until we rejected moral degeneracy. Your body is shrinking tax revenue, your body is kindling. In my inbox, in the submissions to legislation, in their speeches to parliament, on their posters, on their billboards, people referred to abortion as infanticide. They repeatedly and earnestly said that there was no difference between most abortions, which take place before nine weeks without surgery, and the murder of a child. I always found it jarring that these people, who described embryos and teenagers as children, refused to interrogate why having a child might be untenable for someone. If they believed this was murder, would they not be concerned that this woman with a killer's instinct, forced through legislation or neglect to carry the pregnancy to term, would then have a child?

Jacqueline Rose argues motherhood should be 'the central means through which a historical moment reckons with itself' and that mothers can contribute to our understanding of public and political space by dint of being mothers. Actual infanticide has always been instructive – the higher rates in poverty-stricken regions tell us where parents don't feel they have food for another mouth while the clusters of female infanticide show us where women are devalued so much that girls are unwanted. In Toni Morrison's novel *Beloved*, her protagonist Sethe, a runaway slave, slashes her infant daughter's throat as their capture is imminent. 'It ain't my job to know what's worse,' Sethe says of the choice between slavery and death. 'It's my job to know what is and to keep [my children] away from what I know is terrible. I did that.'

Sethe was based on the story of Margaret Garner who, when interviewed by journalists and preachers, did not seem like a madwoman. She reportedly kept saying, 'No, they're not going to live like that. They will not live the way I have lived.' Morrison said in 1987 that her character Sethe did 'absolutely the right thing' but that 'she had no right to do it'. 'I think if I had seen what she had seen, and knew what was in store, and I felt that there was an afterlife – or even if I felt that there wasn't – I think I would have done the same thing,' she said. 'But it's also the thing you have no right to do.' Not all choices made by mothers are acts of maternal love or logic, that blanketing permissiveness most often sought by and granted to white, well-to-do mothers, but even choices that might seem unthinkable to an outsider are made by a human being who knows the truth of her own life so far.

The politicians and organisations who claim abortion is infanticide, who are hellbent on intervening in a pregnancy to the point of birth or shortly after, have never been at the forefront of reforming the structures that make mother-hood impossible for many women. Many anti-abortion politicians have blocked social security payment reform and gendered violence prevention funding while support-ing policies that make life less safe and more precarious for marginalised mothers and their children. They are not campaigning to improve parental leave or wages or make childcare more affordable, and they refuse to support greater access to abortion at the earliest gestation but endorse detaining a toddler in an offshore prison. The disinterest in the welfare of a child beyond the womb is instantaneous.

The stories I wrote in the month leading up to the only comment our current prime minister has ever made about abortion access were like many I had written before, highlighting how bodily autonomy still varied on location, income and luck in encountering a benevolent medical professional. That month I wrote about women in regional areas who were trying to access contraception and abortion when the only doctors in town were religious and obstructive, their waiting rooms adorned with Christian iconography. I wrote about the only national postal abortion service shutting down, leaving women with even fewer affordable privately run options because public access was still a postcode lottery. The gynecologist, well past retirement age, who ran the service at a loss after selling his house wearily told me, 'For the first time in my life, I won't have to be on-call 24 hours a day.' I wrote about how women were crossing the border from New South Wales into Victoria just to find a GP to prescribe them RU486, which had been legalised years earlier and was supposed to be made widely available but the federal government had done little to ensure it was.

That month I wrote about how in South Australia women were having to travel into a major city to a particular hospital to take these two pills, safer than Panadol, to end a pregnancy rather than being able to in the privacy of their own home like women in other states because of an archaic quirk in a 50-year-old law.

I wrote about Sophie, a woman in regional New South Wales, who was about to leave work and drive six hours and stay overnight at a hospital because every hospital near her house had refused to accept her as a patient. She had taken RU486 but the second pill, which expels the pregnancy, had not worked. She could not believe that she was going to have to take sick leave and book a hotel to complete a procedure more than a thousand women in Australia did every week. She needed a D&C (dilation and curettage), an operation that every obstetric and gynecological ward in the country performs every day, whether for a spontaneous or induced miscarriage. 'Whose values and morals does this woman have to abide by?' her doctor, who had been trying to get her into hospitals locally, asked me, his voice breaking down the phone line. I did not publish an article about it but around that time, the doctor called me again while he was in the midst of dealing with another woman who'd had a failed medical abortion in a regional area and needed a D&C. She was waiting anxiously in the emergency department of her large local hospital. They would not admit her as a patient. I am still not sure if it was obstruction by a staff member or an unwillingness to be involved in the aftermath of an abortion while the procedure remained in the state's criminal code. Her doctor was increasingly anxious that they would only see her once she was at great medical risk. It was not until I had called repeatedly and sent media requests to the head of the ward, asking for their policies on who was eligible to be admitted for a D&C, that she was quietly admitted. A situation so tenuous that the threat of bad publicity could change it.

That month I wrote about Olivia, a single mother also in regional New South Wales who had an IUD inserted at her local hospital and then found out she had been pregnant when they gave it to her. The hospital refused to deal with the situation by terminating the pregnancy or removing the IUD and sent her away with painkillers, despite warning her that there was a high risk the device would perforate her uterus because she was pregnant. Every doctor and nurse she dealt with was panicked, she said, but they said it wasn't enough of an emergency to operate until something more drastic happened. Her mother took a day of carer's leave and drove her to a private clinic interstate. The woman paid $540, money saved for her son's first holiday, for the abortion and IUD removal.

In other words, it was an unremarkable month but it explains the situation, from which things have only shifted slightly since, and a point in time where the opposition party felt compelled to make a major election promise to improve sexual and reproductive health in Australia. Labor had pledged to help fix the glaring long-acting reversible contraception and abortion access issues in the country. I tried to engage with the government on this promise, and whether they would offer anything remotely similar, with little success. The government did not want to talk about it. Its own sexual and reproductive health election promise was almost non-existent apart from a chunk of money allocated to an organisation teaching the only family planning practice endorsed by the Catholic church (the Billings method).

The prime minister was taking press on a tour of Australia's notorious offshore detention facilities on Christmas Island, which he was planning on re-opening. A reporter asked the prime minister about Labor's abortion policy. The prime minister said he was very disappointed the issue had even been raised ahead of an election, which he said was typically a 'politically charged context'. I watched this man standing in an island prison for a press conference that was estimated to cost taxpayers $2,000 a minute, dismissing something his party had politicised, as too political to discuss. 'I don't find that debate one that tends to unite Australians and I certainly am not going to engage in the political elements of that discussion because frankly, I don't think it is good for our country,' he said. Data was released weeks later, before polling day, that confirmed what previous surveys had shown: that the majority of Australians, including the majority of voters for his government, believed abortion should be more accessible. It was not divisive. He won the election and nothing changed.

The burden to fix these issues returned to the family planning organisations, medical professionals advocating for their patients, and the few state politicians working to update the law to help them do so. After the election some religious organisation received a million dollars to tell couples what we have known for half a century now, that cervical mucus is a signal of fertility. Meanwhile, a clinic in Victoria stopped taking women travelling from New South Wales and these patients then had to make a 500-kilometre round trip to Canberra for a surgical abortion.

What divides a political party does not necessarily divide a state or country. Anti-abortion Senator Barry O'Sullivan once told me you didn't have to be a 'Rhodes scholar' to know where his party stood on the issue. 'Many in the party and outside would like to lock [pregnant women] up and bind their arms and say, "no abortion could occur",' he said. Polling showed Queenslanders overwhelmingly supported a woman's right to choose, yet every single member of the state's Liberal National Party vowed to vote against the first bill to decriminalise abortion and the second time around, it passed with only three of their votes after members were told their preselection would be threatened if they supported the bill. In New South Wales, a similar thing happened – polling repeatedly showed community support for decriminalisation but religious members of the government threatened to topple the premier over her support for the bill. These antics did not represent most voters' desires. I often wondered what the government would do if it had to confront patients on a case-by-case basis as I had. But the only time I saw this in action it was horrifying.

My colleague Hannah and I wrote in 2018 about a pregnant refugee held on Nauru who had extreme genital mutilation, sustained before she was detained there by the Australian government. She had been in detention since 2013 and wanted an abortion on the grounds that the pregnancy would be harmful to her mental health while in detention. The government's lawyers turned up to court to argue over the degree of her vaginal opening in order to prevent her accessing healthcare in Australia. They argued because her mutilated genitals had been partially unstitched, she did not need to be flown onshore for specialist care or an interpreter and could instead be flown to Taiwan. After spending taxpayers' money to go to court and argue about the extent to which a woman's labia was unstitched, the government lost as specialists testified in her favour.

To write about abortion is to hear constantly from people who know what is going on and to hear nothing from people who can change it. It is to hear versions of the same truths from patients, gynecologists, obstetricians, counsellors, surgeons, frontline domestic violence workers, volunteers and lawyers who repeatedly offer you their expertise and to hear meaningless jargon from government departments. When the status quo denies people the choice to end a pregnancy, those who maintain it are complicit.

I read through hundreds of submissions to the inquiry into the first piece of legislation to decriminalise abortion in Queensland in 2016. There were many arguing for abortion to remain a crime — one asked lawmakers to imagine if Beethoven's mother had had an abortion, another said women were having abortions because they would rather pay for cable TV than nappies, and many compared safe and legal abortion to the Holocaust or to slavery. 'Choosing to be sexually active and risk becoming pregnant these women already exercised "control over their own bodies",' one submission said. 'Now indeed they do have a duty to exercise the control of their own bodies by giving birth.' Another said a woman's body was property and abortion was most akin to breaking a lease. 'The room/womb is let and a souls' agreement has been struck between landlady and tenant/un-born.'

The message was always clear: the maternal archetype for those opposing abortion was a selfless virgin and now thousands of wayward women had gone and brought sex and self-interest into it. However, this hypothetical hypersexualised, or if they were feeling generous, sexually victimised, modern woman had a shot at redemption, in motherhood. Every religious lobbyist I met made it clear that something like forgiveness awaited those who continued the pregnancy. If you don't take absolution, well, you've chosen damnation.

Dr Alexandra Doig, an anti-abortion GP in Brisbane, once gave me a list of alternatives to abortion. Her hypothetical scenarios were not ones I had encountered – a woman who had an abortion because she did not want morning sickness, another who had been unfaithful to her husband, and a pregnant child who had been sexually abused. She gave adoption as an option for most of them and in the case of an unviable pregnancy, she said the woman should be induced, the foetus born prematurely and palliated.

Doig believed the priority for the pro-life movement was 'protecting life at its earliest stage' but for pro-choice activists it was 'sex without consequences'. She said domestic violence was a 'flow-on effect' of sexual liberty and that decades on from the introduction of contraception, 'we now have to teach all children how to identify a pedophile on the street or in their own homes'. I appreciated that she had said the quiet bit loud. In the hours of political debates I had sat through on abortion, some into the early hours of the next day, no one mentioned sex. It was always hovering above the conversation – sex before or outside marriage, sex with strangers and, importantly, sex for pleasure, not procreation.

I have written stories about women whose partners sexually assaulted them and refused to use contraception, flushed their pills down the toilet, one smashing a hormonal implant in her arm, another ripping out her IUD. I spoke to doctors about what they offer women whose partners would turn violent if they knew they were using contraceptives – hormone progesterone discreetly injected, a hormonal IUD with the strings cut short or a copper IUD if he wants proof of menstruation. The ways in which pregnant women are coerced into keeping pregnancies they want to discontinue goes beyond the physical obstruction outside clinics. Reproductive coercion can include contraceptive sabotage, pressuring another person into falling pregnant, continuing a pregnancy, or ending a pregnancy, or forcing a person into sterilisation. It can be so subtle sometimes you wouldn't know how to spot it.

47

I spent the day at a crisis pregnancy centre, linked to vocal anti-abortion politicians and religious lobbyists and marketed as a 'place to pause' before making a decision about an unplanned pregnancy. Behind the Tiffany-blue café serving tea and pastries there were two ultrasound machines, used by a volunteer nurse, who told me, 'My standpoint is that life begins at conception.' Unlike at all-options services, these scans are not diagnostic but a tool to help achieve one outcome. This place did not help people navigate the often complicated path to an abortion or fund terminations for those without means. They existed to support parents in keeping their pregnancies, providing 'pre-decision counselling' and 'congrats starter packs' as well as pram and car seat fittings and 'mummy must-haves' hospital kits.

'I have never met a woman who hasn't regretted her abortion, whereas I've never met a woman who has regretted having a child,' the organisation's chief executive told me. 'Women have fears of the material requirements that a baby might bring into their scenario, so usually it is not pregnancy that is the problem but other stuff around it.' She showed me a storage room that was packed with donated cribs and strollers. If you wanted to continue your pregnancy and had no money, this place would be helpful. If you were trying to access an abortion and thought you had found support, this place would be hell.

*

I have seen how reproductive health needs are prioritised according to fertility, a quality that declines with age. This is not unique to older women – trans men and pre-menopausal infertile women have their own unique struggles – but in my work I have most closely observed the neglect of cis women past their reproductive prime.

I reported on the legal fight between Johnson & Johnson and women who had been implanted with trans-vaginal mesh for prolapse or incontinence. The court, as did a Senate inquiry into the devices from all brands, heard from women, mostly in their 50s and 60s, who were experiencing chronic pain, inability to exercise, sit or sleep normally. They were unable to have pain-free vaginal sex due to adverse impacts from the mesh including in many instances the polypropylene device eroding through tissue and into other organs. At that point, I had interviewed a woman who was suicidal living with complications from mesh, a woman whose husband was pierced by the device after it pierced through her vaginal wall, and a woman who spent tens of thousands of dollars putting her daughter who has special needs into care while she used all of her annual leave to fly to the United States to have the mesh removed after four corrective surgeries in Australia had failed. A video of a mesh insertion was tendered as evidence and played on multiple screens. We watched a series of metal tools plunging into sensitive pieces of tissue, knowing that for some women this piece of plastic would ruin their lives. The judge, a woman, remained stony-faced. The complainants in the courtroom moved uncomfortably in their seats as another incision was made, a knife into an apricot.

In the Senate inquiry into multiple mesh products, women testified that they were repeatedly ignored by their doctors, who appeared disinterested in helping women who were too old to have sex for procreation, have it for pleasure. The women were in some cases told to 'just have anal' sex. Half of the women who experienced adverse physical and psychological side effects after receiving a vaginal mesh implant also suffered a relationship breakdown after the procedure. I wondered whether their pain would have been taken more seriously if menopause did not exist.

I interviewed a 22-year-old woman who had two children and was pregnant with her third. She had been on an implant and then the mini pill and condoms the entire time, but her contraception had failed her thrice. She had gestational diabetes with each pregnancy and was determined not to have a fourth child. She had been referred for a consultation to have tubal ligation but no doctor would consider sterilising her because of her age. 'I was reduced to tears by a medical professional who has no compassion whatsoever,' she said.

She told me a specialist asked her, 'What happens in ten years if one of your children passes away?'

The woman told the doctor she did not need the option to 'replace' her children, she needed to ensure she

50

did not have a fourth. A doctor from the hospital agreed to give me a comment for the story and suggested the woman try a different contraceptive or that her husband get a vasectomy. I thought of each decision this mother had made every day to keep her children fed, clothed and alive without intervention. And yet this final decision, to risk having another child again, was not considered hers to make.

I began to understand how patients can be reduced to something not quite sentient, a set of organs to be fiercely preserved while they could reproduce and ignored once they couldn't.

'I've never had an abortion,' I correct a friend. They'd assumed I had because, they said, I had barely reported on anything else for years. The implication buried in the assumption, which was made by others, was personal attachment. An obsession with your subject matter is what makes a good beat reporter but none of the men I knew who had distinct reporting rounds would have their dedication mistaken as such – the court reporter must have been a victim or perpetrator of a crime, the business journalist must have a giant stock portfolio, the industrial relations reporter must have once been unfairly dismissed. I felt embarrassed. Did they think this is a sad kind of solipsism? Had I not turned down every opportunity to give my personal opinion on abortion until I had finished reporting on it full-time? Had I not repeatedly interviewed people on all sides of the debate? Had I not presented the facts as clearly as possible? Was the expertise of the doctors I interviewed also compromised? I thought of Caroline de Costa, the first woman to become a professor of obstetrics and gynecology in Australia and a regular expert interviewee of mine. The first autopsy she attended as a student in Ireland was a 23-year-old unmarried woman who had died as the result of a backyard abortion. Her uterus was so butchered it fell apart in the pathologist's hands. Does bearing witness to this compromise her 40 years of clinical experience?

I realised this obsession with your specialty was only personal, even pathological, if you were a woman writing about issues that predominantly affected women. What does personal detachment and objectivity look like when you are a woman reporting on the pain of other women? I have always found opinion columns parading as journalism dishonest but if you have made a genuine and good faith attempt to cover the complexity of an issue so fraught, what is the value in denying your interviewees' pain? What is the value of denying your own in reaction to it? Many of my interviewees cried. What is the purpose of pretending I didn't also cry sometimes once I'd hung up the phone? Does our humanity, do our bodies, make us worse journalists? I think the vitriol I received would have stung in a specific way if I had terminated a pregnancy, but I don't believe an abortion would have made me worse at my job. I once worked on an investigation with another journalist who had survived a rape as, statistically speaking, many journalists would have. She taught me to offer victims and survivors as much agency as is possible in how their story is told. Choice has been taken from them, don't make them feel like everything is once again out of their control. I ask if they would like to know which quotes will be used, the likely headline and the framing of the article. I tell them what time the article is likely to be published and send the link. I ask what pseudonym they might like. This journalist's life experience made her, and in turn me, better not worse at the job.

A well-meaning man with decades more experience than me encouraged me to change my focus to something 'harder-hitting' before I was pigeonholed as a journalist who only wrote about 'women's stuff'. I did not know how to say there might not be anything more political than the regulation of a body by the state without appearing too attached to my work. There was so much I could have said about how hard it should have hit him, how hard it had hit me. I understood he thought I had written myself into a corner not through professional dedication but gendered obsession. Eventually I agreed that I had in some way boxed myself in and cut myself off. I had sacrificed something I didn't know how to name.

I didn't have the words yet to say I believed it was motherhood.

*

At the time of writing, Western Australia is the one remaining state yet to pass legislation to create a safe-access zone around abortion clinics prohibiting protests within a certain distance, but when I first began writing about abortion, most jurisdictions had no such measures. Many patients I spoke to had been harassed on their way in. A single mother, experiencing violence and undergoing radiotherapy in her uterus, who couldn't afford to travel interstate and found herself encircled by the religious picketers outside Albury's only abortion clinic. They carried rosary beads and signs emblazoned with dead foetuses. She told them about her medical situation and they told her the pregnancy was God's will. A Chinese–Australian woman who discreetly recorded a 'sidewalk counsellor' offering to help her with her immigration, legal and visa status if she did not enter the clinic. A woman splashed with fake blood, those handed plastic foetal dolls, a sexual assault survivor photographed by picketers when she got back into her car, a nurse who had to comfort a patient when a protester told her four-year-old son that mummy was about to kill her sibling.

Kathy Clubb became the face of a renewed fight between religious groups and lawmakers and health professionals over safe-access zones. Clubb was the first person charged, convicted and fined for breaching the zones around clinics in Victoria when she handed a patient and her partner a pamphlet. The mother of 13 would later appeal her case all the way to the highest court in the country, arguing that the zones themselves were unconstitutional as they impinged on her freedom of political communication. This one woman, and Graham Preston, were together threatening the legality of the zones in all states, and they had the financial backing of the Australian Christian Lobby, who had identified the cases as 'strategic'. Attorneys-general across the country intervened, making submissions to the court against Clubb and arguing that trying to deter a person from making a personal and private medical choice was not political communication just because abortion had become politicised. She lost, but before she did, Clubb wrote a lengthy blog post about me which she also posted on her Instagram. It was titled 'Dear Gina, You're Helping Women Kill Their Babies'. The stock image was of a distraught woman sitting in a car, her hands covering her face. Presumably I'd helped her to murder her child.

Clubb and I had corresponded for a few stories and our interactions had always been polite. It was a shock to realise she thought of me at all. Her diatribe focused on a story I had written about what was inside the bags anti-abortion picketers were handing patients entering an abortion clinic in Perth. The bags contained tissues, a single sachet of tea, a Starburst fruit chew, a single Mentos, plastic rosary beads, argan oil hair treatment and, most significantly, multiple brochures heaped with misinformation which redirected women with unplanned pregnancies to anti-abortion crisis pregnancy counselling. One brochure from the church-funded Pregnancy Problem House falsely claimed abortion increased 'self-destructive behaviours' and the risk of breast cancer. Another wrongly claimed medical abortions were illegal in Australia. 'Now I don't blame you for promulgating these falsehoods,' Clubb wrote to me in her article. 'You also haven't seen the glazed-over look of the women who come outside after their abortion.' This was true, I did not regularly station myself outside clinics like she did. However, I had spoken to at least as many women about their abortions as religious picketers like her had. An interviewee who had read the blog post told me, 'Of course women looked glazed-over ... I had just been sedated and someone is coming at me with a pamphlet full of prayers.'

As the only reporter writing about abortion regularly in Australia and with an international, mostly American, readership, I found myself a target for people like Clubb. By then I had been sent prayers, bible verses and a rape threat, but something about her article, the boldness of the accusation in its title, derailed me. I felt sad and exhausted and completely isolated. Everyone I told dismissed her as an outlier, a voice from the fringes, a stranger. I didn't know a single person who would understand how I felt. I wanted to write about anything else.

She has the same name as my mother. My mother, who attended pro-life rallies at university. My mother, who believes life begins at conception. My mother, with whom I fell into an uncomfortable silence over my job. It was easier not to talk about it. The first time I mentioned my reporting, she defended protesters, explaining they were only trying to help and they should have the right to do so. She saw the eventual successful enactment of safe-access zones in our state as Clubb did, a loss for freedom of speech. It felt as though it did not matter how many women told their stories, they would always be murderers and I would always be aiding and abetting them, complicit in something burning with shame, smoking with sin.

I was raised a Catholic but casually so. I went to church on Christmas and Easter, attended scripture classes and had a fleeting devout phase around the age of ten, when I began the sacraments of initiation. I would kneel before a shrine of Mother Mary I had resting in the unused fireplace in my room and thank Jesus for my good health before bargaining with him to reunite my parents, help my brothers and make sure my sister passed her law exams. In my First Reconciliation, in which you have to go to confession for the first time, I confessed to the priest that my bedroom was messy. He gave me ten Hail Marys. I wore a white dress and patent leather shoes for my First Eucharist, in which you are given the body of Christ and his blood, a sip of red wine, for the first time. Then finally I had my Confirmation, in which you are given the gift of the Holy Spirit and the name of a saint. I chose Frances. I stopped believing soon after that.

More than a decade later, I arrived at one of Sydney's older courthouses to begin covering a murder trial for a newspaper. There was the same solemn hush of church, the same deference to a man in robes. It was a high-profile case, in which two men were accusing each other of pulling the trigger, and I had arrived slightly late. The wooden benches were long and shiny like pews and as I moved towards the row allocated for journalists, without thinking, I genuflected. I locked eyes with the judge as my knee kissed the carpet, my face warming. I shot upright and shuffled into my seat. He smirked, a TV reporter stopped chewing her gum, bewildered, and a juror looked at me sympathetically. Until I was about to go into emergency surgery, this was the only indication that something of Catholicism had left its mark on me, a tattoo I found as permanent as I am.

As I sat on the edge of the hospital bed and signed the papers to have my ovary cut out, I felt scared but unsurprised. I couldn't express, even to myself, how inevitable it felt that my reproductive system would fail me. I observed the strict binary of what a mother could and could not be, unchallenged, even by my own reporting. This was the bolt of lightning I had been waiting for. It struck me for living in sin, for wanting a career, for not marrying, for using contraception, for writing about contraception, for writing so much about abortion, for being unsure about motherhood. If there was a God, would He not punish me for fact checking His disciples in multiple parliaments? For framing motherhood as anything other than destiny? For my ambivalence? For my criticism? My body was kindling. Two hundred millilitres of blood spilled into my pelvic cavity, clouding the ultrasound. I knew it was an unhinged,

58

potentially morphine-induced thought but motherhood felt like a mirage, unreachable to a woman like me even if I should want it. *Where is your bodily autonomy now?*

Maybe religion has branded even non-believers, or maybe the stories we tell ourselves about women and the choices they make have less to do with theology and more to do with power. It took me a long time to realise that not every person opposed to abortion was holding rosaries. Most of them were just clutching pearls. Religion explained the hallucination of retribution but not the inadequacy I felt. How fast I found myself capable of reproducing lies about my capacity to reproduce. I became to myself the infertile woman as she has been historically – an object of suspicion, self-interested, uncaring, cold, unfeminine, scheming, more inclined to practise witchcraft.

Hippocrates thought women fell ill because their uterus was moving around the body, searching for moisture. This 'wandering womb' stalked like an animal wanting to be inseminated, Terri Kapsalis writes, adding that if it went towards the throat, the woman would lose her voice, choke or cough, and if it got stuck in the ribcage, she might have difficulty breathing. In Ancient Greece, magicians prescribed hysterical women amulets to heal their wandering wombs but as Kapsalis notes, the mischievous uterus was thought to relax into its proper place in pregnancy. 'The triad of marriage, intercourse, and pregnancy was the ultimate treatment for the semen-hungry womb,' she writes. 'The uterus was a troublemaker and was best sated when pregnant.' By the 19th century, hysteria, derived from the Greek *hystera*, meaning womb, was thought to be a psychological rather than purely physical disease. In 1873, a Harvard professor wrote that women should not pursue higher education because they might become 'irritable and infertile' if blood travelled to their brains instead of nourishing their uteruses. The idea persists: if the womb isn't being used for its God-given purpose, it wreaks havoc. People told me that falling pregnant would ease the symptoms of endometriosis. '*Only for nine months,*' I thought.

I want to feel in communion with other fleshy beings, united by the vulnerability and brevity of our shared existence on this earth, impelled to face every existential threat as one. But in many places, we are still women before we are human. I am scared of the ways in which motherhood might enforce and cement my gender. This is what happens when you nail an identity to the womb – arms just tubes ending in ovaries, legs descending straight down like a cervix, hopes and dreams expanding only as the uterus does. She nurtures, she supports the growth of others. Woman as womb makes fertility synonymous with functioning, makes procreation purpose. Woman as womb sidelines all the women without wombs – transgender women, cis women with Mayer-Rokitansky-Küster-Hauser syndrome or those who have had hysterectomies. Woman as womb insists family must be made there, as though people don't foster, don't adopt, don't make room at a table for a stranger who becomes a relative.

The Most Important Job in the World

I have spent so much of my life feeling indignant about being, as Denise Riley says, 'positioned antagonistically as a woman-thing'. That gendered self-consciousness has, Riley writes, 'mercifully, a flickering nature'. I am reminded in flashes, usually by other people, of myself as a woman-thing. Rarely is it enjoyable – a burst of glowing solidarity with other woman-things, an unexpected flash of gratitude for being socialised to express my feelings. More often it is a feeling that your body is illuminated by an inextinguishable and volatile flame – a bolt of fear as a man yells at you out of his car window, a fiery flush when a boyfriend's mother asks if you feel maternal, the searing grief of reading about another murder at the hands of someone she trusted. The stinging reminder that your body isn't quite yours.

2

Climate change

'Why would anyone have kids?' my boyfriend muttered, looking down at his phone screen, smouldering tangerine with footage of flames tearing through our state, razing hundreds of homes. We were lying in front of a fan, learning of the destruction as we do all modern disasters: incrementally, pulling down to refresh feeds while news outlets kept pushing articles onto our home screens.

Months before the coronavirus outbreak reached Australia, we were already acclimatising to a kind of dystopia in which face masks were selling out as people rushed to protect their lungs from the smoke billowing through much of the country. Fire and emergency chiefs agreed that bushfire season, which killed nine people and destroyed more than 3,000 homes, was made longer and deadlier by climate change.

The years of my childhood were divided between delighting in summer and waiting for it to begin. When I learned the seasons were reversed in each hemisphere, I imagined the kids on the other side of the world feeling in May how I would in November – giddy with impatience for months of running around at the beach, picking frangipanis to put in bowls of water and behind ears, collecting seashells and threading my brother's fishing wire through them to make necklaces, eating yellow nectarines and frozen cartons of pine-orange fruit drink and shaking the sand out of my library books before returning them. I was unbothered by the sweat, the mosquitos or the sunburn. The bushfires and extreme temperatures seemed to me as isolated and infrequent as any other horror flashing across the 6 pm news bulletin. The days were long with daylight and possibilities and still I wanted these months to stretch on indefinitely. I vowed that when I was an adult I would hop between hemispheres, chasing summer so I would never have to wear a cardigan again. I would have wished for what is now our reality – Australia's summers have become twice as long as our winters. Now that I have experienced heat as oppressive, I feel only a sheepish trepidation for December.

On 30 December 2019, volunteer firefighter Samuel McPaul died when extreme winds lifted the back of the ten-tonne truck he was travelling in, encasing it in a tornado of fire. His wife was pregnant with their first child. Two days later, a couple of hours into the new decade, Dr Steve Robson drove through Australia's capital city, Canberra, as it recorded its worst air quality on record. The air quality index reading peaked that morning at 7,700 – more than

23 times the hazardous AQI of 300. His headlights barrelled through the smoke as he made his way to hospital to deliver a baby. When he flicked on his spotlight to examine his patient, he noticed this beam of light was also cloudy with smog. 'This baby was born into bushfire smoke,' he told me afterwards. Robson reminisced about the deliveries two decades earlier, when he experienced an unadulterated joy in chaperoning new life into the world. It was a different time, when parents believed their children faced abundance and nothing was insurmountable. We had just survived the Y2K bug, he remembers, laughing. 'There was a sense that people could solve big problems but that sense seems to be very ephemeral, it has evaporated,' he said. 'Every single mother-to-be and every single dad-to-be I've seen today has expressed to me anxiety about what the future holds for the child they're carrying.'

I interviewed Melbourne obstetrician Dr Nisha Khot, who said pregnant patients close to their delivery date were asking about whether they should induce labour due to the bushfire smoke, which unbeknownst to either of us would a week later cause the worst air quality in the world. 'They're asking, "Is my baby safer inside or outside of me right now?", they're asking, "What does this mean for my baby's growth?" and "Do I need extra ultrasounds?" and I have to say, "I can ultrasound scan but it won't pick up any effect of the bushfire smoke that may or may not occur because there isn't a test that picks that up" . . . Those are the difficult conversations.'

People start families throughout wars, recessions and ecological degradation but millennials are statistically more likely than those who came before us to be anxious about climate change, perhaps because we can no longer deny it. A survey of thousands of millennials across 13 countries at the end of 2020 showed even a global health and economic crisis couldn't shift climate change and protecting the environment as their top concern, above unemployment, healthcare and disease prevention, and income inequality. Half of all millennials and Gen Z interviewed said they believed society had reached a point of no return and that it was too late to repair the damage caused by climate change, and when asked if current and future efforts to protect the planet's health will be successful, only 40 per cent of millennials expressed optimism, a number that had dropped eight whole percentage points in a single calendar year.

'Maybe it's the case that every generation has felt themselves at the end of the earth, on the brink of disaster, though I suspect never with as much evidence as we have now,' Léa Antigny writes. She describes a 'fundamentally physical, bordering on erotic desire to feel pregnant', to sense new life growing inside of her even at a time when rising temperatures will affect the timing and seasons of our natural world. 'I want to be reduced by love to just bodies and to grow a family from it. But what comes after that?' Antigny realises that she might be 'rich enough to shield her descendants', as the *New York Times* put it, from the incoming impacts of climate change. 'Is the fact of my privilege reason enough to forge on? I want to be able to answer why beyond simply saying, I want to, and I can.'

I am still deciding, but if the answer was yes, could I find and hold my why or would I allow it to become eclipsed by a how? How on earth? How on *this* earth?

My friend Alex says that he has always imagined himself as a father but climate change has become the biggest factor in deciding whether or not he and his wife will have kids. 'Some days I'm really hopeful, like at the start of spring I sit in the backyard with Mary and we're surrounded by flowers in bloom in a garden that cannot be stopped and the bees are thriving and everything smells glorious and hopeful and I think we are going to have a dream life,' he says. 'And then the bushfire season starts.' Their simmering worry always boils down to the question of whether existence is a gift or a curse. 'Are we leaving behind a world that is better or are we kind of cursing someone to deal with the impacts of whatever it is we have done, or if not done, been mildly complicit in?'

Friedrich Nietzsche described how Silenus, friend of the god Dionysus, declared the best thing for men is 'not to have been born, not to exist, to be nothing'. At a picnic, my friend with a toddler says to me, 'No one regrets being born.' It is this tension, strung with guilt, that hangs above me and other people I know who are undecided about having children. Although I do feel it in waves, it is hard for me to authentically buy into the deep-throated antinatalism that has captured many of my peers. Even in my darkest moments, I can't bring myself to accept the period between birth and death is so perpetually painful and sparingly joyous that I'd never have jumped aboard.

It is hard to predict precisely how the cataclysmic shifts in our climate will cause pain and steal joy from the next generation, and so when Alex and his wife do let themselves imagine a life with kids, they feel ill-equipped. 'How do you prepare? How do you prepare for having children and then how do you prepare children for whatever the world is going to be next?'

I want to know how I might temper the ambient dread about the climate for long enough to evaluate whether I wanted to foist another carbon footprint onto the aching earth and, I believe more significantly, foist these increasingly untenable conditions onto another human. If I choose not to have children and the climate becomes the biggest feature in that decision, I need to be able to explain to myself why I believed the prospect was too much to bear even on the days where I am not concerned with rising tides and blanketing smoke. If I choose to have children I need to have a justification that feels less fragile than the foetus growing inside of me. And so, I sought out people who were forced to stare directly into the future of the climate crisis. I found them swinging, just as I was, between hope and fear.

Joëlle Gergis is an award-winning climate scientist. She is a lead author on the Sixth Assessment Report by the United Nations Intergovernmental Panel on Climate

Change (IPCC), a body that assesses the scientific basis of climate change so governments around the world can develop climate policies. 'I'm watching the things we talk about theoretically actually unfold on a planetary scale, that is the stuff that freaks me out,' she says. 'There is no analogue in the geologic record for where we are. We are kind of off the map . . . We have never had 7.6 billion people on the planet altering the earth's surface and the chemistry of the atmosphere and the ocean on this scale.' When we speak, Joëlle has just worked through the weekend to meet an IPCC deadline and she's knackered. The workload is gruelling but Joëlle wants to know that at this 'important juncture' for turning emissions around, she did what she could. Joëlle is an expert in Southern Hemisphere climate variability and, I soon notice, an expert in loss – the potential, the inevitable and the irretrievable. 'Kids that are alive today are going to see the Great Barrier Reef deteriorate and die, and kids that come after that are going to learn about it in the same way we watched grainy archival footage to learn about [extinct] Tasmanian Tigers,' she says.

I went to the Great Barrier Reef as a child with my dad. It was surreal, borderline unreal: the tiny tiger-striped clownfish weaving in and out of translucent anemones, the manta rays soaring down steep coral shelves, the dopey green sea turtles, most of whom were at least twice my age, disinterestedly drifting past as I gasped into my snorkel. The tanned skipper, a marine biology student, explained the noise pollution and disruption the boat was wreaking on the coral atoll was a small price for the reef to pay if everyone on the boat developed an appreciation of and desire to protect it. At that age, my understanding of environmental catastrophe was a series of disjointed incidents in which criminal corporations or careless citizens harmed innocent animals – dolphins starving to death, their noses caught in plastic bottle rings, harpooned whales bleeding out on the deck of a ship, sea birds black and greasy from petroleum oil spills. These individual battles to save distinguishable species were sad but tractable. I didn't understand how changes in the ocean temperature, runoff and pollution and overexposure to sunlight would stress, bleach and eventually kill this dreamlike ecosystem.

There have been five mass global bleaching events of the Great Barrier Reef since I was born. If I had children, they would never experience the beauty of what should have been guarded as a national treasure but the loss feels bigger than the reef itself; after all, most generations enjoy something the next do not, even if coral hosts a quarter of all marine fish. It feels like defeat. We didn't preserve this UNESCO World Heritage site from rising sea temperatures, we didn't guard a 46,000-year-old sacred Indigenous site from mining companies, we didn't protect the 250 hectares of tropical rainforest (previously thought to be non-flammable) from the flames. There is so much to lose and not enough political will to save it in time. Joëlle uses the word 'planetary' eight times in our conversation to describe the scale of the climate crisis. Each time, I feel my stomach drop.

The Most Important Job in the World

As Joëlle watched flames destroy more than 20 per cent of Australia's forests in a single bushfire season, she felt as she had when her father died – a deep awareness that something so loved was now gone. Grief. 'The planet has always been able to cope with us, hasn't it?' Joëlle ponders. 'We had that "Save The Whales" iconic species type conservation but now we are talking about the planetary system really starting to buckle and that to me is completely different. Climate change is taking the worst, most extreme aspects of Australian climate variability and just amplifying it.' Joëlle says that the 2019–2020 bushfire season will be average by 2040 and cool by 2060. 'This will absolutely barrel through everyone's life, whether you're holed up in your home from regular 50-degree summer temperatures or your property becomes flood-prone and uninsurable because you live on the eastern seaboard or you're paying $13 a kilo for bananas because the farmers who grow our food keep having crops devastated.'

Joëlle does not have children but she does not judge anyone making this decision and says self-flagellation is unproductive. 'I'm not sure if it is helpful for people to feel even worse about something that is already a very fraught and deeply personal question because then the issue becomes very heavy. I think if you are bringing kids into the world, you just have to go into it eyes wide open knowing that they are not going to have the life you had,' she says. 'I think it needs to be really firmly grounded in the reality that it's going to be a more dangerous world, particularly if we don't turn things around.'

When I did my first round of bushfire media training as a cadet at a newspaper, the instructor explained that a fire front could move faster than any of us could run. Once you got close enough, you could die before the flames even touched your skin. If you got out of the car and tried to run, there was a 100 per cent chance of dying but if you lay down in the backseat and covered yourself with a heat-proof blanket, you had a less than 10 per cent chance of surviving, albeit with burns all over your body. I knew I would run. I knew in the moment I would believe I had a chance of surviving it and that this conviction would be the certain death of me. When I get off the phone to Joëlle I think about how I might keep my eyes wide open as she suggested. I think about how I might actually ground myself in a terrain that will always be as rickety as politicians and executives allow it to be. For days I read as much as I can about everything we discussed: unbearable heat, emissions timelines, planetary boundaries, cascade of dominoes, king tides, coral bleaching, devastating crops, rainforest loss, tipping points. I softly place my forehead next to my keyboard and close my eyes.

As the summer approached in 2020, Rebecca, a GP in a regional town, discovered babies born to her patients who were pregnant the previous bushfire season were coming early and underweight. The placenta is normally pink and healthy and comes away easily during birth but these were grey and grainy, as they are in pack-a-day smokers, requiring an operation to remove them. 'One patient brought in photos and I know what placentas look like, I've seen a lot of births during my obstetrics training, and this one was just horrifying,' Rebecca tells me. 'The placenta is a magic filter that feeds our next generation and we have these smoke particles lodging in there.' She explains that drugs in Australia are grouped into categories (A, B1, B2, B3, C and D) based on how safe they are to take during pregnancy and there is an extra category (X) for drugs that have such a high risk of causing permanent damage to the foetus that they should not be used in pregnancy or when there is a possibility of pregnancy. 'A pregnant woman during these summer bushfires, breathing in that toxic smoke, is effectively breathing in a category X and that is alarming to me,' she says.

Rebecca lives on the property she grew up on. The dam that supplied the farm with water for 60 years is completely dry and the summer berries now come in spring. Fires burned the farm out a few seasons ago and she has since had to evacuate twice with the kids and dogs while her husband stayed to defend it from flames. 'I have been in that position holding a six-week-old baby and racing out of the house while a bushfire comes over the hill,' she says. 'For three months of the year, actually now six months of the year, we have generators ready, we have fuel ready, we have bags packed ready to go at any moment.' Rebecca is passionate about preventative health – she speaks in factories and at pubs to men in lower socioeconomic demographics about reducing alcohol, smoking and blood pressure. 'Sometimes I wake up in the middle of the night and think what is the point of doing all this work every day to save people from having heart attacks if we're all going to be living in a world that is two degrees hotter by 2050?'

Air pollutants have been linked to premature birth, low birthrate and miscarriage in the first trimester. One study showed that a 20 microgram per cubic metre increase in nitrogen dioxide (NO_2) resulted in a 16 per cent risk of miscarriage. In Sydney, where I live, the NO_2 increased by 122 micrograms per cubic metre during the 2019–2020 bushfire season.

A friend and I sit at a café, estimating the ideal month someone would conceive to avoid smoke damage to a foetus. 'I guess in like March, so the baby comes during summer and you're inhaling the smoke when it is most developed and almost ready to be born?'

It is disorienting to imagine the dangers of climate change reaching a baby when they are yet to feel the safety of their parents' touch.

I lost all sense of time when I spoke to Chris, an evolutionary and conservation biologist, about his deep desire to start a family despite witnessing devastating biodiversity loss every day. There is an urgency to his work – mapping the consequences of rapid environmental change for native animals – but he logs it on a fathomless timescale that makes most species, including humans, look like an imperceptible last-minute arrival on earth. 'Do I think about climate change? Constantly, because I study any rapid changes or novel scenarios that shift the playing field and totally disrupt species,' he tells me. Chris is currently helping to develop a model that can better calculate and predict what proportion of animals die under different fire scenarios, a project that came about when scientists realised they didn't have a way to accurately guess the animal death toll in that 2019–2020 bushfire season. The latest imperfect estimation is that three billion animals were present in the areas that burned. 'A lot of the animals in Australia are actually adapted to fire and they have a whole lot of responses to deal with it and so if you suppress fire, you change the distribution, abundance and composition of species in the landscape which had all been maintained by Indigenous Australians for thousands of years [before colonisation interrupted it].'

These animals long ago learned to burrow lower or climb higher when they sense fire, then a carefully managed phenomenon, but scientists are wondering how native species will cope with the increased severity and frequency of Australia's new fire regime. Any significant environmental change discharges a starting pistol in a race between adaptation and extinction. 'Extinction will win if the change is too quick, and the problem is changes are happening at a rate that is unprecedented,' Chris says, before correcting himself. 'Well, there have been multiple global extinctions across the planet.'

As we talk, I fleetingly group humans in with our treasured marsupials and reptiles for their ingenuity and resilience – a comforting comparison – until I remember that we, settlers, are both the perpetrator and the victim, the invading and the endangered species; we are lighting the match and then fleeing the fire. Over the past 20 years, Indigenous community–based landowner groups in Australia's very fire-prone north have used traditional fire management practices – burning early in the dry season instead of suppressing fires that ignite late in the dry season, which is a post-colonial practice that creates bigger and more severe fires. I wonder how these practices will be maintained in unprecedented heat and aridity. 'I am currently living in a place that is on the edge of what humans can tolerate in terms of climate,' Chris says. 'It is insanely hot here and any level of warming will make an already intolerable place beyond tolerable.'

Chris doesn't think people should deny themselves a family because of climate change. 'It is like when people can't really appreciate evolutionary change because it happens on a scale that is incomprehensible to us,' he says. 'This problem is incomprehensibly big and it is more than any individual can take on and while I think people should live responsibly, I don't think they should be racked with guilt for choosing to have a child which is a totally natural decision to make.' His desire to be a father feels more than biological. 'I can't really describe it but there is an innate desire in me to have [fatherhood] as an experience and I don't know how I know this or why I feel this way but I feel like I could make a child's life happy and fulfilled and good,' he says, his voice changing in a way I can't understand in the moment. 'This is ridiculous but you're the first person that's going to hear this . . . this has become much more, ah, practical than theoretical because we just found out that [my wife's] pregnant.'

Just as Chris finds it hard to articulate the scale of fathomless evolutionary timeframes, I struggle to capture in words the bolt of celebratory joy that crackled through the phone line. In between his peals of laughter and my blaring exclamations and repeated congratulations, I later hear him on the tape in stoked disbelief say quietly, almost to himself, 'Yeah so . . . I *am* going to be a father.' Hope itself needed to become more practical than theoretical. 'My feeling is even when things are difficult, it is better to be alive than not to be.'

In 2017, before she became the Australian Capital Territory region's Commissioner for Sustainability and the Environment, Dr Sophie Lewis was expecting her first daughter and working on an academic paper examining when current record-breaking extreme temperatures in Australia would not be considered exceptional but average and eventually cool. She was emailing back and forth with another author on the paper, who was also pregnant. 'One of the sentences I had written in this really dense verbose scientific language was that by 2035, it was going to be far hotter and [the other author] wrote back a comment in the Word document just saying "oh fuck". It just cut through this great excitement we were experiencing personally for these long-fought-for girls who were about to join our families because in 2035, they would be in high school. Everything just collapsed into one. There was no scientific research and babies on the side. It was just this one thing and I knew this wasn't some time period in the future that was separable from our kids.'

Two years later, Sophie became the ACT's Scientist of the Year and the bushfires hit, filling her home with toxic smoke. 'I find the air quality indescribable but it is incomprehensibly bad,' she remembers. 'It feels immediately horrifically bad for your physical health. There is something powerful psychologically about smoke that sends your body into a panic that this isn't safe and you shouldn't be here.' Smoke was rolling into Canberra from the New South Wales south coast as fires cremated the first place Sophie took her daughter on holidays. 'The homes of friends and the homes of animals were burning and that smoke was blowing into our home and I couldn't keep my daughter safe from that.'

As the New Year ticked over, Sophie left her partner in Canberra and took their daughter interstate to Tasmania to give her fresh air. Each night, Sophie would put her daughter to bed and cry. 'I think it was a deep grief for what was going on environmentally and it was a period of deep reflection on what I was doing and where I was putting my time and energy. I felt like my scientific work was really of little value you know? Decades of clear and consistent science has not prevented [the bushfires] from happening and there was no sign that any of that was going to change,' she says. 'Why do I leave my kid to go to conferences to talk about this? Why do I work 60 hours a week when I get paid for 28 hours a week for something that is not having any impact on the world?' When Sophie returned to Canberra at the end of January, 80 per cent of Namadgi National Park, some 60 kilometres from their home, was consumed by another fire. Her family watched gigantic smoke clouds rise by day and roaring flames crest over the mountains at nightfall. This was the eighth consecutive month Australia had been fighting fires. 'I think my discomfort was turning into a feeling of betrayal of our lives and my daughter's future because we have done nothing to prevent this in terms of climate mitigation and adaptation.'

Sophie has always known that she wanted kids. She says she would have 25 if it was possible for her and the planet, but she has just one and another on the way when we speak. The family has endured three consecutive miscarriages. 'We had all of those concerns regarding what [the decision to have children] meant for those kids and also for the world and being so aware that there is an enormous environmental cost to having kids in the life that we live,' she says. The decision was made repeatedly. 'When you don't have the core biological components to create a child, it is a very active decision and there is so much thought that goes into how you will do that and the practicalities and that prompts all those decisions around what are you doing and why?' she says. 'Because we had immense difficulty having our children we were revisiting that time and time again and affirming that was what we wanted when we had those natural exit points we could have had.' Sophie describes her fear around climate change as relentless but her hope as stronger and more stable. She spends a lot of time in schools with children and is impressed by how capable and knowledgeable they seem. 'I feel more consistently hopeful and invested in that optimism and then I guess I have these big waves of worry and dread and all those negative emotions which are quite oscillatory,' she says. 'There is such hope and joy in babies and young children. It isn't particularly fair on them to rely on them to generate those feelings.'

In his book *Notes from an Apocalypse*, writer Mark O'Connell reflected on this burden, one his small children are now carrying, to be a beacon in a dark world. He wondered whether he had selfishly acquired a new sense of optimism about the world at the expense of his son, who he protected from the news cycle. 'But there are times when it seems that we are protecting him, and protecting ourselves, from a much deeper and more troubling truth: that the world is no place for a child, no place to have taken an innocent person against their will,' he writes. 'Given the world, given the situation, the question that remains is whether having children is a statement of hope, an insistence on the beauty and meaningfulness and basic worth of being here, or an act of human sacrifice. Or is it perhaps some convoluted entanglement of both, a sacrifice of the child – by means of incurring its birth – to the ideal of hope? You want to believe that it is you who have done your children a favour by "giving" them life, but the reverse is at least as true, and probably more so.'

It is uncomfortable to admit but in those moments when I see the appeal of early motherhood, I am drawn towards this eternal presentness of children. It is self-interest – I'm reaching back to a time before I could see any rottenness in the world, before I was aware of my own fallibility, before I lay awake at night obsessing over my collisions with all that I found painful in the universe and in myself, pressing my fingers into these bruises, mauve with shame and fear. A proximity to children tugs your gaze beyond your own navel and into the present moment – following their eye line and experiencing with them the novelty of things you take for granted, answering the disarmingly specific questions about how things work, lunging to prevent bumps and falls, and the sheer relentlessness of cleaning and feeding. I can't hear my own neuroses above the noisy *nowness* of children.

Jenny Odell believes that we live in a culture that puts novelty and a cancerous rate of unchecked growth before all that is cyclical and regenerative. 'Our very idea of productivity is premised on the idea of producing some-thing new, whereas we do not tend to see maintenance and care as productive in the same way,' she writes. Is it fair to produce, primarily for myself, a human object of hope to live on a planet I have done little to care for and maintain? Am I drawn not just to their *nowness* but the sparkle of their *newness*?

Somehow, this impulse towards the immediacy of children sits adjacent to an anxiety about what the world will look like when they are adults. I know that to have a child involves extending yourself into a hypothetical future, where they will have to survive in a world you have left.

In September 2019, as the fires began in Australia, millions of children around the world went on strike from school, demanding action on climate change. In Australia, there were three times as many people marching as in the United Kingdom, which has five times our population. 'There is no planet B' their signs, replete with wonky crayon globes, reminded us. The yelling, the chanting, the laughing, the uncompromising belief in the most basic of human rights. I let myself believe these tiny marchers would save us, even though our fear, not our hope, was what they were demanding. 'Adults keep saying, "We owe it to the young people to give them hope." But I don't want your hope. I don't want you to be hopeful. I want you to panic. I want you to feel the fear I feel every day,' Greta Thunberg told those gathered at the World Economic Forum in Davos in 2019. 'And then I want you to act. I want you to act as you would in a crisis. I want you to act as if our house is on fire. Because it is.' Yet, as Thomas Whyman has pointed out, Thunberg was addressing the business and political elite gathered in the Swiss Alps, not us. 'Their hope, she is suggesting, is toxic – like bad air, choking out the stuff that we can breathe,' he writes. 'We need, as Thunberg points out, to found an almost entirely new world – just in order to survive. But they, who benefit from the existing order of things in such disproportionate magnitude that they might realistically expect to survive a massive crisis in the provision of basic resources, have a vested interest in our never doing so.' Our hope is rooted in the potential of transforming our world, Whyman insists. The hope of the very elite is founded on the likelihood that we cannot.

When two volunteer firefighters, both fathers aged in their 30s, were killed after their vehicle hit a tree while on duty, it was revealed Prime Minister Scott Morrison was not in the country. Australia's equivalent of the stunning photograph of three men golfing against the backdrop of a cartoonishly towering wall of flames that went viral during the Oregon wildfires was of our prime minister secretly holidaying in Hawaii while the country burned. He smiles, the sun setting softly behind him. His left hand is making the shaka sign – *hang loose, chill out, no worries, mate* – while his right hand is locked into a firm bro shake with a grinning tourist. He would offer that same hand a few weeks later to an exhausted firefighter who had just lost his house to flames. He responded, 'I don't really want to shake your hand.' Morrison nonetheless awkwardly picked up the man's limp left hand before walking away.

When he was quizzed about why he had taken a holiday while the country was on fire, he compared his decision to that of a plumber who had to decide between seeing his kids or taking on an extra plumbing contract. 'These are things you juggle as a parent,' he offered. Morrison, who earns more than half a million dollars a year, or 7.5 times that of most plumbers, then said he wasn't going to give in to people who wanted Australia to do better on climate action. 'I never panic,' he said. 'The urge to panic . . . is not something I'm ever intimidated by or distracted by.'

Dr Lara Stevens, a Melbourne Sustainable Society Institute research fellow, lay awake, anxious, after finding out she was pregnant with a girl. 'I just started thinking about how she will navigate the world and what kind of world there was going to be there for her at the other end of it all,' she says. 'I was watching Greta Thunberg's speeches at that time and feeling like "what an inspirational figure" but also the gravity of what she was saying . . . It was a personal crisis and a planetary crisis hitting me at the same time.'

Lara wrote a one-woman live art piece *Not Now, Not Ever* on one of these panicked nights while pregnant. She later performed it on stage, breastfeeding her newborn daughter and reciting philosopher Georg Wilhelm Friedrich Hegel who stereotyped men as animals and women as 'peaceful' plants unfit for political action.

I tell Lara that I have often thought about whether we would perceive the natural world as needless, infinitely giving, a bountiful enigma there to meet our limitless material needs, if we had imagined her as a Father Nature instead. 'By casting nature as feminine, it means the natural world is always a second-class citizen,' Lara tells me. 'It is there to be raped, to be beaten, to be eaten, abused or otherwise manicured or beautified for our pleasure.' These ideas can be found in eco-feminism, which emerged in the mid-1970s alongside second-wave feminism and environmental activism to make connections between the domination, degradation and exploitation of nature and that of women. 'Eco-feminism challenges the narrative that we are above the natural world, that we are its masters and we have to control it and use it for our gain, that it is there for us and our pleasure and it is going to feed us and clothe us . . . eco-feminists have been saying we're come of the earth and we're interdependent with it and if we don't start addressing that mistreatment it will bounce back on us,' Lara, who has written extensively about the movement, says. 'The attitudes we have towards nature have a common ground with the way we treat women but also other marginalised communities like poor communities, Indigenous communities and LGBT communities.'

This is not just metaphor-making. Every week a new study emerges that shows the dangers of global warming are disproportionately shouldered by minorities and dis-advantaged communities. An examination of more than 32 million births in the United States found pregnant women exposed to high temperatures or air pollution are more likely to have premature, underweight or stillborn children – one study found high exposure to air pollution in the final trimester of pregnancy was linked to a 42 per cent increase in stillbirth risk. These risks were higher for African–American mothers, who the authors said were more likely to live close to power plants and other sources of air pollution and less likely to have air-conditioning in their homes or live in neighbourhoods with green spaces that might keep temperatures down.

Lara believes we need to make a 'wholesale change' as a species from an atomised, individualistic and consumer-driven way of living to something that considers the interests of the community and the planet. The question of whether or not to have kids changes across borders, she says. 'I think it is really important to bring race and class and nationality into the discussion and recognise that if we are having a child in the US and Australia they are going to use on average 15 times more resources during their life compared to a child of the developing world,' she says. 'That is going to impact the decisions we make about how many children we have and how we live. A lot of people, and myself included as a privileged subject, are not going to like how our lives are upended in some of those changes that we are going to make but we can't keep growing at the level of affluence we have.'

In 2016, helicopter crewman David Key was awarded a bravery award for his rescue role in the 2009 Black Saturday bushfires, in which 450,000 hectares burned and 173 people were killed. I interviewed him at the time about the day he put the lives of four strangers, a couple of horses and a dog named Poncho ahead of his own when he descended into the hellish flames enveloping their property. He disconnected himself from the chopper to save his two colleagues hovering above and bundled the family into a car. One of the children held her horse's reins out the window as it galloped alongside them. 'It was amazing the other animals that were running along with us: deer, wombats and kangaroos,' David said. He told me that the family and the 'Noah's Ark' worth of wildlife that followed them all made it out of the flames and to the safety of a paddock. I remember absorbing this image as some kind of poetic proof of the democratising function of disaster, that we are all just animals running towards a field. But we are not. The burden of climate change has and will continue to fall unevenly, as it has since the 2009 Black Saturday and as it will beyond the 2019–2020 Black Summer. And yet, somehow, the allocation of responsibility has been skewed when it comes to the question of family planning.

In November 2019, more than 11,000 scientists from around the world declared a 'climate emergency' and outlined six policy goals to address it, the last of which was to stabilise or 'ideally' gradually reduce the population, in part by making 'family planning services available to all people'. Alongside fossil fuel replacement and ecosystem restoration, helping people family plan can seem like a benign notion but even after writing hundreds of stories about how dangerous limiting abortion and contraception access is, it made me deeply uncomfortable. I don't think there is a way to set population control as a 'goal' without emboldening people who have an opinion on which populations should be controlled. Unlike more familiar factions of the political far-right, eco-fascists acknowledge the climate crisis is underway but offer genocidal solutions – rarely designated for countries with higher per capita emissions like Australia – to what they see as the scourge of overpopulation, industrialisation and immigration. A few months before the scientists announced their policy goal, 51 people at two mosques in Christchurch, New Zealand, were murdered by an Australian man and self-identified 'eco-fascist' who was a direct inspiration for another mass shooting three months later by a man in Texas who wanted to 'get rid of enough people' to make our way of life 'more sustainable'. Environmentalism has long been misappropriated by white supremacists.

'Historically, population growth alarmism coupled with eugenic ideas about who is worthy of reproducing has led to a painful global legacy of coercion and abuse,' writes social and behavioural scientist Kelsey Holt. Earlier in 2019 I met with a global reproductive healthcare provider, MSI Reproductive Choices, the backbone of abortion provision in Australia and in much of the world, each year preventing millions of unintended pregnancies and unsafe abortions and averting tens of thousands of maternal deaths. At this lunch, they told me about how their expansion of family planning services in Asia and the Pacific was helping girls into education, addressing teenage pregnancy and reducing maternal mortality rates. A Cambodian employee explained the immeasurable impact this has had for women in her country. Then, the two white women talked about how women and girls in these regions were most vulnerable to the impacts of climate change but could be 'empowered' through reproductive healthcare with 'solutions'. They gave me a pamphlet about their work in the Asia-Pacific that explained how family planning programs were an incredibly cost-effective 'climate-change mitigation strategy' by slowing population growth and therefore lowering emissions. Whether in an innocuous brochure or a horrifying manifesto, the issue of population control ends with a proportioning of responsibility. If it was really a conversation about emissions, family planning organisations would focus almost entirely on increasing the contraceptive uptake of women in high and upper-middle income countries, where 86 per cent of CO_2 is emitted globally. The research team for Our World in Data, based at the University of Oxford, found even if we added several billion additional people in low-income countries, where fertility rates and population growth are already the highest, global emissions would remain relatively unchanged. This is not to shift the burden of one uterus to another but to acknowledge that it has ended up entangled in our reproductive choices at all.

The childless woman has long been a symbol of selfishness, an uncaring wench incapable of putting someone else first. The climate crisis has created the conditions for a new kind of shame to grow, in which self-sacrifice looks like a family with no or very few children. It isn't just spread by extreme groups like the Voluntary Human Extinction Movement, which calls for humans to stop breeding so the

Earth's biosphere can return to good health, or the Birth-strikers, who refuse to procreate until the climate crisis is addressed. Most mainstream outlets have published multiple articles reminding us that the worst thing you can do when it comes to carbon emissions is to have a child. It is worse than having a car, boarding a plane, eating meat or failing to recycle, we are told. An acquaintance posted a photo of his newborn baby on Twitter and below my 'congratulations' someone replied, 'It's an inescapable fact that earth is overpopulated. When are we going to stop saying "congratulations" to those who had a choice, and start asking, "how dare you?"'

We know that more than a third of all greenhouse gas emissions since 1965 can be traced to just 20 fossil fuel companies. The idea that we should abridge our desires for the size of our families and communities before transform-ing our energy systems is peculiar, and yet I know if I was to have a child, I would be scrambling to shrink its footprint before its feet even hit the ground.

In the 1950s, the packaging industry in the United States conspired with beverage brands like Coca-Cola to move the problem of litter from themselves, the creators of disposable packages, to the consumer via what became a wildly popular 'environmental' campaign, 'Keep America Beautiful'. Americans stopped asking where these disposable goods came from and began policing themselves and each other for where and how these unsustainable materials were being disposed. The litterbug, not the litter producer, became the antagonist. This kind of corporate green-washing, in which the individual is responsible for cleaning up a structural mess, is well underway when it comes to greenhouse gas emissions and it has worked on me. What does resistance look like when you see yourself as a single consumer rather than a citizen in a collective?

Veronica Milsom's voice is recognisable to most people my age in Australia as the former host of our youth radio station's drive time program. It was strange hearing her in the middle of the night, raspy from lack of sleep as she tended to her baby's leaking cloth nappy, a reusable and more environmentally friendly alternative to the disposable plastic version. 'She's wet her onesie all the way through because of these stupid *fucking* nappies that don't work,' Veronica croaked on her podcast 'Zero Waste Baby', in which she tries to raise her second daughter to have as little impact on the environment as possible. A few episodes in, after months of endlessly changing and washing cloth nappies, Veronica learns it might have all been for nothing. Cloth nappies reduce waste because you're reusing them but because Australia is so addicted to coal for power – it accounts for more than 70 per cent of our electricity generation – that another environmental burden was created by the washing and potentially drying of so much laundry. If you washed with hot water and tumble-dried it might be even worse for the environment than disposables.

'No!' I exclaim stupidly to no one. I had caught Veronica's infectious enthusiasm and forgotten the systems within which she was making these decisions weren't aligned with her wish for a cleaner planet.

'I think it is important for us all to take personal responsibility for the part we play in helping the planet but I would love it if our federal government showed any sort of leadership when it comes to implementing big changes towards a future of renewables,' Veronica tells me. 'The current state of politics is abysmal and embarrassing.' The emissions gap – the difference between what countries have individually pledged to do to reduce greenhouse gas emissions and what they need to do collectively to meet the Paris Agreement goals – has widened by four times in the past decade, my most fertile. We need to act faster to achieve the same reductions. The podcast reaches its natural conclusion – Veronica considers whether having no baby at all is better than having a 'zero waste baby' in an interview with a prolific vasectomist.

I ask Veronica about hope, considering even the most ambitious of personal commitments to reduce a new child's waste ended with a contemplation of the child not existing at all. 'It only really hits hard on days when I'm feeling pessimistic about the future of the environment and the idea that humans aren't doing enough to steer this ship around to avoid complete disaster,' she tells me. 'I also think it'd be hypocritical for me to think like that because I was armed with all the same information to make my decision about having kids and I chose yes and I absolutely don't regret it. Having kids is the single best thing I have and ever will achieve. They make me happier than I could possibly imagine and they make me want to be a better person and take care of our planet.'

Ketan Joshi, a clean energy analyst, is defrosting when we speak. He has just cycled home through Oslo's icy sleet after dropping his toddler to childcare. When he arrived in Norway from Australia, he had never cycled but the city had bike lanes from which he could zoom past car traffic and he fell into the habit easily. 'I'm incredibly unfit and I'm a bit scared of cars but these bike lanes are really great and because someone else fought in this collective action in the past, I made this easy individual decision,' he says.

The term 'carbon footprint' was popularised almost 20 years ago by British Petroleum when the oil behemoth unveiled a calculator so individuals could see how their daily activities contributed to global warming. On 23 October 2019, as Australia's bushfires were well underway, BP tweeted: 'the first step to reducing your emissions is to know where you stand. Find out your #carbonfootprint with our new calculator & share your pledge today!' Ketan responded, pointing out BP was the 11th in the world for industrial greenhouse gas emissions and included a graph showing the company's carbon footprint from 1988 to 2015 as similar to that of domestic emissions of the entire country of Australia. If BP was a country, he pointed out, its per capita emissions would be more than 5,000 times that of any other nation in the world. 'Just so you know where you stand,' he wrote to @BP_PLC, adding a winky emoji.

In his book *Windfall: Unlocking a Fossil-free Future*, Ketan makes the point that the average Australian could live in a gigantic house, each of the eight bedrooms permanently air-conditioned, drive two 4WDs and live a wasteful life and still you would never negatively impact the future of our planet as much as a single politician blocking action on climate change or an executive at a company that extracts or burns fossil fuels. It is the realisation of this exact fact about which Ketan feels the most fear and, unlike most people I talk to, he is not worried about a distant date linked to a sea level rise or a degree of warming. He believes it will come before his daughter even reaches high school. 'In the next five to ten years, very novel changes to the biosphere will probably trigger a really violent moment of realisation,' he says calmly. 'This is something that I hold to be a bit inevitable in that there is very little we can do to prepare for it.' The realisation, he predicts, will be a fundamental reconfiguration of how we allocate blame and therefore responsibility. And, he predicts reluctantly, it will be bloody.

'I think the bushfires that happened in Australia made people far more aware of climate change as a threat but it has had absolutely no impact on making people link it back to decisions and behaviours from fleshy beings,' he says. 'You never end up back at the root cause, which is that a bunch of people knew the consequences and they went and did it anyway and that is what caused the novelty and the intensity of Australia's bushfires. If you were to ask someone,

"Hey what is causing climate change?" they would say, "I think it's fossil fuels", they wouldn't say, "I think it's deci- sions made by a collection of politicians, corporate leaders and individuals all contributing to this".'

I think of everyone I know who has stopped using things that produce emissions and reduced the use of things that use emissions to be created. My housemates carefully sorting the recycling into different piles, the vegans, cyclists, reluctant op-shoppers, KeepCup washers. I think about Veronica folding dozens of cloth nappies every night, preparing for another day of mess, I think of all the reading I've done about lifestyle choices – having or not having children, raising them in a wasteful or not wasteful way. Apart from a few cowardly politicians, I have never really thought seriously about the individuals in government or corporations as making lifestyle choices, even though they will have far more impact on the style of life we will all have to adapt to.

Ketan says people will realise this didn't start with atmo- spheric physics or climate science but with people who made decisions and that these decisions will be described as eco-terrorism and geoengineering. 'It is geoengineering when a company like Shell says we are going to discover an oil field, extract it and sell it because they are making a conscious decision fully aware of what the consequences will be on human life,' he says. 'When people get that and when that is widely realised as a consequence of disasters that hit with such frequency and intensity that people realise that could only have been done by people it probably will be perceived as an aggression and reacted to with aggression.' Ketan says this scares him because he has never lived through war, he's only read about it. 'It is probably going to happen between countries and companies and people who remain wedded to the burning of fossil fuels in spite of this wider realisation of this causal chain behind disaster and the people who want that to change.'

I have been speechlessly transcribing for 15 minutes, my fingers tapping while my brain conjures images of widespread civil unrest. I am thinking about the IPCC report which described how a breakdown in food systems would aggravate poverty and hunger and increase 'the risks of violent conflict'.

'I know I sound a bit fatalist,' he says almost apologetically. 'But this is the only thing I keep in my doom bucket because I think this realisation is inevitable but then this anger will fuel not just a youth climate movement but an everybody movement.'

Ketan describes his attitude towards solving the climate crisis as 'infuriated optimism'. His optimism seems to be rooted in potential. 'Australia's potential to contribute to a resolution of this problem is far greater than other countries if it started to export renewables and use zero-carbon energy instead of fossil fuels. It is hard to overstate how much of a positive impact that would have,' he says. Australia's variable environment leaves it particularly vulnerable to the impacts of climate change but we are also uniquely placed to step up to help mitigate them. While 2.8 million petajoules of fossil fuel reserves lie underneath us, above us every year shines 58 million petajoules of the sun's energy, making us a perfect candidate for widespread solar panel use, he explains. His fury is about squandered opportunities to decarbonise and failure to close old coal-fired power stations in Australia when there are zero-carbon, zero-air pollution replacement options. 'The frustration comes not from a lack of effort but from seeing so many easily avoidable losses become losses anyway.'

Ketan shows me a photo of his daughter dressed up in a Christmas costume before we get off the call.

Anger felt like the necessary bridge between delusion and defeat. It took my hand from my brow, where it rested in despair, and off my heart, where it could no longer feel hope, and curled it into a fist. This might seem like useless tinkering, fine-tuning a coping mechanism, cognitive behavioural therapy in the face of an inoperable tumour that will only continue to metastasise your entire life, but I have to believe there is something with more teeth than faith. We won't be sustained by a crippling guilt, curled over seeking redemption in a handful of consumer choices. Unlike guilt, which folds us into ourselves, anger has an object, an other to be held accountable. This should always have been the case in a crisis that was made by humans with power and will only be unmade by humans with power, even if only in numbers. Optimism, after all, might be a luxury good – hope is harder to find when you are trying to protect your family from fire or flood – but resignation, too, can be an indulgence, enjoyed by the luckiest.

I was once pitched a very Silicon Valley story about a start-up that allowed parents to invest in a fund to pay for their adult children's IVF. It was framed as a cheeky way to buy yourself grandchildren. My first thought, an idea with which I would charm no shark nor secure any capital, was that I would think more seriously about having children if my parents' generation could instead prove they had converted their financial luck or political power into political will to address climate change. As JR Hennessy has written, older generations living in the developed world are members of history's most under-appreciated death cult. 'The loudest and most powerful voices when it comes to the future of the planet – the ones with their hands on the levers of power – have a strong tactical advantage: they will be dead before the shit really hits the fan,' he writes. Your contribution to a debate depreciates alongside your stake in it. 'The kids want to win it,' he writes. 'Boomers just want to die before we get to the closing arguments.' I spent too much time indignant at my parents' generation and their favourite media outlets for their climate-change denial. An article published in *Quadrant*, a magazine that notoriously once ran a piece calling for the headquarters of our national broadcaster to be bombed, argued that those on the left are deceiving prophets of doom who are inventing the irreversible impact of human-made climate change because they love the drama of it.

I thought of when Scott Morrison, then treasurer, mocked progressives by bringing a huge lump of coal into parliament, provided by lobby group the Minerals Council of Australia. 'This is coal,' he said, brandishing it as his colleagues chuckled behind him. 'Don't be afraid, don't be scared.' Fear itself has become politicised. Environmentalism is not apocalypticism and there is irrefutable evidence that the climate system is warming. It is appropriate to use language like 'emergency', 'crisis', 'collapse', and 'tipping point'. I do, however reluctantly, agree with the idea that millenarianism – the belief that there is an incoming collapse of society as we know it – is spreading across the political spectrum and there are some people who take pleasure and purpose in it. It stretches beyond the threat of environmental disrepair and into civilisational Armageddon – you can see it on the feverish faces of preppers, high on their own self-sufficiency, preparing for, in their words, when SHTF (Shit Hits The Fan) at which time they can finally assert their unhinged machismo and protect their families. Mary Heglar saw it in all the 'doomer dudes' she met while working at an independent left-wing newspaper as a 23-year-old. These 'climate de-nihilists' were almost always tall white men – 'only white men can afford to be lazy enough to quit on themselves' – in cargo pants, who gleefully declared humans were done for.

I can see the tempting clarity in the doom. Catharsis, the purging and relief from negative emotions, has the same etymological root as Catharism, a medieval Christian religious sect opposed to procreation, a morally evil act as it perpetuated the chain of human suffering in the material world. Both words derive from the Greek *katharos*, meaning pure. I sense it in myself some days, the feeling that there is nothing to be done, and that feeling, no matter how fleeting, feels completely incompatible with having a child. In the same way that I don't fear death like I do dying, I am far more comfortable with the world's mortality than its morbidity, probably because it requires less from me, including the tiresome work of hope-making.

I received a news update that Australia's first satellite to detect bushfires within a minute of their ignition would soon launch. I wondered if that was where we were heading in lieu of treatment. The automated surveillance of our planet's terminal condition. '*I guess we'll just get a bit faster at watching the world burn,*' I thought, retreating into the horror.

The idea of an apocalypse is tempting because it allows us, as Mark O'Connell writes, to vault over the chasm of the future and all that we might do to change it and straight to the end of all things. 'Out of the murk of time emerges the clear shape of a vision, a revelation, and you can see at least where the whole mess is headed,' he writes. 'All of it – history, politics, struggle, life – is near to an end, and the relief is palpable.'

There is comfort in certainty, even in certain demise as it releases us from the responsibility to answer many of the questions we ask each day. How can I help mitigate this catastrophe? Too late. Should I have a child? Don't bother.

But I don't want to be a doomer dude, the kind who, with their 'joyful nihilism', unknowingly convinced Heglar that environmentalism was inaccessible for years until she realised that because warming happens in degrees, there was always something to be done. 'We, quite literally, have no time for nihilism,' she writes. 'I've never seen a perfect world. I never will. But, I know that a world warmed by two degrees Celsius is far preferable to one warmed by three degrees, or six. And that I'm willing to fight for it, with everything I have, because it is everything I have.' Heglar doesn't need a guarantee of success and neither should we. 'Even if I can only save a sliver of what is precious to me, that will be my sliver and I will cherish it,' she writes. 'If I can salvage just one blade of grass, I will do it. I will make a world out of it. And I will live in it and for it.'

In her book about narcissism, Kristin Dombek says to endure the selfishness of others is to witness your independence laid bare as a myth while watching their gaze turn away. 'The selfishness of others is the feeling of time moving past you; what history feels like,' she writes. 'The selfishness of others is the feeling of the center shifting, the knowledge it was never under you.' It is learning the history of the complicity of governments and corporations in the chaos we will continue to witness in our natural world.

Dombek feels her own selfishness as absence. 'The absence from my life of the trash I leave behind, which becomes the structures into which others must live, the broken hearts, the warmer air, the slower fish, the rising ocean: whatever I

101

do not feel, that to others becomes the shape of their world.' She discards a cigarette into a snowbank. 'There is time, still, to move backwards into the future of others, gazing at the disasters we are leaving behind and trying to mend,' she writes. 'My selfishness will be invisible until spring, when the world warms, the snow melts, and someone else turns the corner to find this littered street.'

I read about a landscape architect who will use oyster reefs to mitigate the storm surges and tidal flooding caused by climate change by slowing the movement of water. 'There's no more natural nature,' she tells the *New Yorker*. 'Now it's a matter of design.'

It isn't our ideas that make us optimists or pessimists but our optimism or pessimism that makes our ideas, according to the Spanish philosopher Miguel de Unamuno. If the scientists I spoke to didn't believe that we could, that we had to, avoid the iceberg, they wouldn't be toiling in the bowels of the ship, keeping the boilers at steam. They wouldn't be recording, mapping, fighting and convincing. Regardless of whether or not I become a parent, I do not want to be absent. If I remain childless, I will use my anger and hope more meaningfully, beyond the random donations and the second-hand shopping and the infrequent rallies. If I did become a parent, I would pledge not to absorb the guilt and shame of the institutions who should feel crippled by it, nor assume my kids would pick up the slack of political action as our parents have done.

I will be here for summer, no matter how endless it feels.

3

Reproductive justice

I am suspicious of motherhood for what I have been taught to believe it is – the ultimate expression of womanhood. When your gender is the primary, or the only, weight under which you have felt oppressed, there is fear of solidifying it. Why would you further associate yourself with what is deemed less valuable? I can feel my own reluctance, and that of women like me – white, university-educated, non-disabled, middle-class – to have a child if parenthood might mean relinquishing the political, sexual and social power that has allowed us into places and conversations historically reserved for white men with money.

Who is encouraged to be a mother? Who is trusted as a mother? Who is protected as a mother? When suffragists first conceptualised 'voluntary motherhood', decades before marital rape was a crime, they were doing so to liberate a type of woman whose right to be a mother is rarely challenged. Their experiences were never universal and yet refusing motherhood remains a paramount right that main-stream feminism strives to protect above other social and reproductive liberties.

What does it really mean to fear motherhood as a white middle-class woman? To wonder if I will become invisible before I imagine myself surveilled. To resent the domestic realm when I am not strictly designated to stay there. To picture my eros fading while other bodies are mythologised as hypersexual. To see myself depoliticised as a mother before I do criminalised. I knew the questions I would ask on the page were not borne proportionately by all women but I wanted to understand why I felt pregnancy and parent-hood would interfere with the place my body occupies in the world. If I'm going to sulk about a loss of power, of control, of agency, I need to explain how I have them in the first place. If I'm going to talk about reproductive health, I need to speak of violence as well as care.

'Hiii Auntie Gigi.' My niece's head floats into frame as we video call on the morning of her first day of school. She shows me the red ribbons in her hair, her new school shoes adorned with love hearts and rainbows and her chequered school dress, so cartoonishly oversized my stomach cramps from what I can only attribute to cuteness. 'I might not make any friends,' she says quietly, a statement I know is a question. I reassure her, desperately wishing I could instantly catapult interstate to do so in person. Sometimes I wonder how my sister can function alongside this immobilising love. This feeling, this raw protectiveness and glistening delight, this soreness and sweetness I feel watching my niece grow and interact with the world.

This pure and private feeling is stolen from families in this country every day.

Naomi Williams should have been taking her son to his first day of school the same week my niece began kindergarten. 'At the end of the day, she should still be here and her little boy should be starting school,' her mother Sharon tells me. In the early hours of New Year's Day in 2016, Naomi, an award-winning disability worker and Wiradjuri woman, died. She suffered a cardiac arrest caused by an overwhelming sepsis infection while en route back to the emergency department that had sent her home the previous day with two paracetamol, 34 minutes after she got there. She was 22 weeks pregnant.

In 2018, I reported on part of the coronial inquest into Naomi's death. We listened to evidence that Naomi had been to Tumut Hospital 18 times in the eight months leading up to her death, repeatedly complaining of symptoms including vomiting, nausea and abdominal pain. In most cases, she was given anti-nausea medication and fluids, offered drug and alcohol and mental health counselling and sent away. The inquest heard that Naomi had tested positive for *Helicobacter pylori*, a stomach bacteria that can cause pain and nausea, in June 2015, and in September that year was diagnosed with excessive morning sickness. The inquest heard that Naomi had used cannabis to alleviate her symptoms but the drug and alcohol reviews had found she was not dependent on that or any other substances. 'They had already made their mind up [that Naomi was a drug user],' Sharon says. 'There was drug abuse and whatever going on in the community and they painted her with the same brush.'

Two months before her daughter's death, Sharon wrote to the head of nursing staff at Tumut Hospital explaining that her daughter needed a specialist referral for her ongoing symptoms of vomiting, nausea and pain, and that the repeated referrals to drug and alcohol counselling were adding to her daughter's distress. 'They have tried to apologise to me but I will never forgive them,' Sharon says. 'They just dismissed Naomi like she was a nobody. It was absolutely disgusting. The amount of times she presented to the hospital and doctor would have to be a red flag for anybody.'

The inquest heard Naomi's partner Michael explain that the day she died was not the first time she went to Tumut Hospital 'begging for help'. 'During the time she was pregnant, she went there again and again for her nausea,' he said. 'She would come home and tell me how tired she was of just being ignored – just being turned away. She felt like nobody was there listening to her.' Michael said the pain would never leave him, that he was barely holding things together since Naomi died in front of him and his 12-year-old daughter. He said life was 'almost perfect' three years earlier when he was waiting for the birth of their son and they were talking about getting married. 'That dream was shattered in an instant on New Year's Day when I watched the love of my life and my baby boy die in front of my eyes,' he said to a silent courtroom. 'I just wanted to take a moment, so the court and all the lawyers and hospital staff here understand what that feels like, when the light in your life has suddenly been taken away and all that's left is empty darkness.'

Sharon says she tries to focus on the good parts of her life and writes things down when it all becomes too much. 'I've still got stuff here of hers that I have to unpack and I struggle with letting go a bit,' she says. 'We're getting there slowly and teaching the boys to be strong and proud, to speak out when something isn't right. They know and I know her story will flow through them.' Sharon sends me photos of the healing garden she has built as a tribute to Naomi.

The state's deputy coroner, Harriet Grahame, told the courtroom she herself would not have been treated as Naomi had. 'Naomi Williams went to a doctor many, many times and never got a specialist referral,' she said. 'If I look at it from my own experience as a middle-class woman in the eastern suburbs of Sydney, my perception is I would have got a referral and that is my strong perception. I would not have gone in 18 times and not gotten a referral.'

I remember frantically transcribing this as she voiced what I had been thinking all week. I was the same age as Naomi had been and I knew this never would have happened to me. The court heard that Naomi had already decided she would have her baby interstate, where she could access a local Aboriginal Medical Service because, as her mother relayed, they would better 'hear what she was saying'. I could not imagine my medical history, my pain, my mother's email having been ignored.

Grahame ruled that while the nurse and midwife on duty could not have known Naomi's symptoms were a sign of a life-threatening bacterial infection, her care at Tumut Hospital was inadequate and Naomi had 'reduced expectations of care' in the hours before her death. 'I am satisfied that had there been more curiosity and inquiry involved by those caring for Naomi at the time of her presentation, a fuller picture of her condition may have emerged,' Grahame said. Naomi should have had an assessment of her pain and medical history and 'at the very least' a doctor should have been called on for further medical advice.

During Naomi's inquest, Yin Paradies, a professor of race relations, was cross-examined about the implicit racial bias in hospitals which meant Indigenous patients received worse levels of care. He said they had 30 per cent fewer procedures than non-Indigenous patients even accounting for location, socioeconomics, gender and age. He explained Indigenous patients were discharged from hospital, against doctors' advice, at a rate five times higher than non-Indigenous patients. This was due to six reasons: 'racism, lack of cultural safety, issues of miscommunication, issues of mistrust, family and social obligations, loneliness and isolation'. Outside the court, he spoke to another journalist and myself and elaborated: 'Historically, we had the stolen generations ... in hospitals, there has been a history of forced sterilisation and babies being taken and so on'.

As with so many Black deaths, no one was criminally charged, no one was fined, no one was personally held responsible for Naomi's death. While an inquest found systematic failures, recommendations were only to the specific local health district, namely to make sure an Aboriginal liaison health worker could be available 24 hours a day and to improve the employment of Indigenous people as health workers to reduce danger in an unsafe system for Aboriginal patients. The recommendations do little to address the racism from which Sharon could not protect her daughter. Sharon believes if Naomi wasn't racially profiled, she would have been listened to. 'She would have been taken more seriously and I think they would have checked her medical background, seen her history and sent her straight to a specialist,' she says. 'She lay down and cried, she was anxious. They didn't act on it or treat her with respect. She was put in the corner, put on a drip and left. She was treated like a second-class citizen.' Sharon lists what she wants to change in hospitals after her daughter's death. The demands are painfully modest – for all patients to be listened to, for all patients to be treated with respect, for all patients to know that if they have presented multiple times, they will be attended to. 'We are the experts in our own bodies and we know when there is something not right.' The infection that killed Naomi was treatable with antibiotics.

*

Layla F Saad says white supremacy is 'an ideology, a paradigm, an institutional system, and a worldview' white people are born into. 'Whether or not you have known it, [white supremacy] is a system that has granted you unearned privileges, protection, and power,' Saad writes. 'It is also a system that has been designed to keep you asleep and unaware of what having that privilege, protection and power has meant for people who do not look like you.' It is white privilege to be able to ignore the role of race in my reproductive choices and in motherhood. I have spent too much time worrying how my experience of pregnancy or motherhood would entrench my own oppression and not urgently considering how they would solidify my presence in places where other women are mistreated.

Now that I am wondering how I would plan a family, I see how narrow my definition of family planning has been. There is reproductive health – on which I have reported, fact-checked and myth busted. There are reproductive rights – on which I have documented the legal restrictions and legislative changes around abortion and contraception. I have not spent much time on reproductive justice, which values not just the right to not have a child but the right to have a child and to parent that child in a safe and healthy environment. It goes far beyond pro-choice feminism and was created by activist women of colour to capture, as academic Loretta J Ross describes, how gender, race, class, ability, nationality and sexuality all intersect to produce a reproductive politics that goes far beyond ending or preventing a pregnancy. 'In addition to supporting the pro-choice movement's goals of protecting abortion rights and securing safe and effective contraceptives, as people of colour subjected to continuous population control strategies, we must fight equally as hard for the right to have children and to parent the children we have,' she writes. There are so many groups of women who seek reproductive justice within violent systems in this country – pregnant asylum seekers we detain in offshore prisons, parents we deny affordable fertility treatments, mothers on temporary visas trying to access social support – but the lasting legacy of who is encouraged to procreate and protected to safely do so in this country begins with colonisation.

Waanyi writer Alexis Wright says that 'since time immemorial' her ancestors managed to survive in fragile environments. 'In the Aboriginal world, we know the apocalyptic realities of two and a half centuries of continual invasion, an invasion informed by the Enlightenment project of colonisation, which has been driving the major environment disasters of the Anthropocene and the harmful realities of globalisation.'

Noongar novelist Claire G Coleman has said that she never intended to pen dystopian novels but while writing a book about the invasion of Australia in 1788, she realised that all novels about this nation's history were inherently post-apocalyptic. All Aboriginal and Torres Strait Islander people were descendants of people who survived an apocalypse when they went from being the total population to just

3 per cent of it. 'These were end times, the ending of a civilisation, of a culture, of a people,' she wrote. 'Many of those who survived the epidemics were massacred, the survivors of the massacres were rounded up, forced into concentration camps, had their culture destroyed and were often enslaved.'

The threat of environmental collapse, economic instability and uncertainty can feel like the end times for those whose lives have for a long time been overflowing with stability, hope and water that runs clear. 'We don't have to imagine an apocalypse, we survived one,' Coleman writes. 'We don't have to imagine a dystopia, we live in one – day after day after day.'

I think fears about pregnancy and motherhood need to be tethered to reality, to a context beyond yourself. The structures inside which I find liberty and safety can be places of violence for other women. The assumption that a woman can, should and will reproduce, though restrictive, is not universal.

White people have always been encouraged to reproduce themselves in Australia. As legal academic Larissa Behrendt has written, ever since British invasion there has been 'a call for the right type of woman to reproduce the nation'. In 1904, a Royal Commission into the declining birthrate in New South Wales delivered its report condemning white women for having fewer children and putting their own comfort ahead of reproducing. This selfishness had struck 'at the welfare of the white race in Australia' and would generate 'a weaker race of Australians', claimed a *Sydney Morning*

Herald article published following the commission's report. The commission had been called in response to the huge decline in the Australian birthrate during the 1890s but it was more an 'ideological exercise' than a 'rational inquiry', as historian Neville Hicks observed. The deliberate limitation of fertility increasingly practised by women in Australia was of concern to everyone from doctors to politicians to clergymen, who feared the social and moral implications. It was clear, in the opinion pieces and letters to newspapers at the time, that population growth through immigration or by increasing the rate of the whole population was not the proposed solution. 'They feared for the future of the Anglo-Saxon race in Australia,' Hicks wrote. This report came during a decade when Aboriginal parents didn't even have legal guardianship over their children in most jurisdictions – their kids were legal wards of the state and so could be torn from families and relocated. It is estimated that up to a third of all Aboriginal and Torres Strait Islander children were forcibly separated from their families between 1910 and 1970 alone. Despite the abolition of many of the initial policies, including that of assimilation, which took children from their parents and placed them in often abusive institutions and taught them to reject their Indigenous heritage, this state-sanctioned removal has not stopped.

It would make me happy as a feminist to write about reproductive rights as a united and equal march towards bodily freedom but as Sara Ahmed says, if talking about racism within feminism gets in the way of feminist happiness,

113

then we need to get in the way of feminist happiness. You can't talk about modern family planning organisations and movements without tracing their undeniably racist roots. 'Failing to recognise how white supremacist ideology affects pro-choice organisations jeopardises our collective ability to defeat our mutual opponents and weakens the entire movement,' Ross writes.

You can pick almost any family planning organisation older than a few decades to understand eugenic influence on the birth control movement. Two letters – the MS in MSI Reproductive Choices – tell a long story about the largest abortion provider in Australia. Marie Stopes was a white founding mother of the reproductive rights movement who has been lauded for defying the Catholic church and opening Britain's first clinic offering birth control advice to married women. She was a classist, racist, disablist homophobe whose proposed eugenics program has been described as 'slightly to the right' of that enacted by Adolf Hitler, to whom she sent a book of poetry in the 1930s. She wanted the 'hopelessly rotten and racially diseased' to be sterilised.

The biggest publicly funded contraception and sexual health service in my state, Family Planning NSW, was founded as the Race Improvement Society and then the Racial Hygiene Association of New South Wales. The third object of its first constitution was to improve the race on eugenic principles. The association said in 1932 it 'openly advocates sterilisation of the unfit' and that a 'good or bad human race does not just happen – it is bred the same as sheep etc can be bred'. They were concerned with preventing venereal diseases and, as historian Sylvia Bell wrote, the 'promotion of racial fitness through premarital health checks'. Family planning organisations at the time received backlash because of contraception rather than their blatant eugenics – population control was accepted in Australia long before birth control was. As historian Diana Wyndham suggests, the eugenics movement was only less active and organised in Australia than it was in other countries because these principles were already enshrined into our legislation and founding ethos. *Terra Nullius*, land belonging to no one, was the concept used by the British government to justify the colonisation of Australia, and the brutal policies that followed were informed by the idea that colonisers were there to 'smooth the dying pillow' for a 'dwindling race' – the oldest living culture on earth, spanning back more than 60,000 years.

The White Australia Policy to restrict non-British migration to Australia was not completely eliminated until the 1970s. As 'custodians of the white race', many feminists supported the White Australia Policy and wanted to preserve white racial purity because whiteness had become the uniting feature of Australian nationalism, writes Aileen Moreton-Robinson. 'The new enfranchisement for white women tied them to increasing the white population,' she writes. 'Unlike white women, Indigenous women were not encouraged to produce offspring.' Maternity bonuses were granted to white women in 1912 and Indigenous women were not directly entitled to maternity allowance until 30 years later.

Just as abortion rights activists in the United States failed to fight against the epidemic of sterilisation abuse of disabled, Puerto Rican, Black, Chicana and Native American women, those in Australia failed to acknowledge these abuses against Indigenous women. Moreton-Robinson has written that Indigenous women want stricter controls over abortions and sterilisation because they have been 'practiced on our bodies without our consent'. She details how Aboriginal medical services in the 1970s and 80s were using Depo-Provera, a contraceptive injection not approved in Australia until 1994. 'It did not work and many Indigenous women became pregnant and suffered spontaneous abortions,' Moreton-Robinson wrote. A 2020 study of factors influencing contraceptive use or non-use among Aboriginal and Torres Strait Islander people found the post-colonisation history of contraceptive abuse enforced upon these women still impacted their decisions. These included the use of Depo-Provera without informed consent as a form of short-term infertility, sterilisation for unexplained reasons or without consent, prevention of reproduction through forced removal of children, and the criminalisation of having children with other members of Aboriginal and Torres Strait Islander communities.

Academics Boni Robertson, Catherine Demosthenous and Hellene Demosthenous wrote a 2005 paper based on stories collected from a yarning circle of Indigenous women, including children of the Stolen Generation, in which the question 'Why can't I be a mother?' was repeated.

The authors point out that debates in Australia about 'reproduction and the national future' questioned the capacity of poor, white women to reproduce but for Aboriginal women, their right to reproduce and mother their own children was 'completely out of the question'. Aboriginal women have always been accepted as 'fit to care for and rear the children of white women' while being denied the rights to mother their own children. The authors wrote that the agendas of so many white women's groups failed to address not only the rape and abuse of Aboriginal women at the hands of white men but the denial of their right to be mothers and theft of their children by the state. '[Advocates] seemed to have ignored the fact that while others had a choice to reproduce and mother their own children, Aboriginal people were being controlled by the state and told what to do as women and as mothers,' they wrote.

Moreton-Robinson writes that for many Indigenous women in Australia, 'motherhood meant having their children forcibly removed from their care' and radical feminists have failed to take that into account. It is not just that white feminists have failed to secure the same rights for Indigenous women – white women in Australia were given the vote in 1902 and Indigenous women were not granted this right until 60 years later – it is that they often colluded with institutions who denied them these rights. 'As beneficiaries of colonisation, white feminists have been able to challenge and remake themselves as white women through the state and other institutions,' Moreton-Robinson writes.

While white women have been gathering power, aspiring for the same lives as white men, 'Indigenous women assert that by working to improve the conditions of impoverished women in Australia, the status of all women will be enhanced'.

The right to fall pregnant, to safely carry that pregnancy to term and to parent free of discrimination and coercion is as important as the right to prevent and terminate a pregnancy without discrimination and coercion. These rights are not valued as they should be by the patriarchy under which we all live, nor by the mainstream feminism that is failing to resist it for all women. Moreton-Robinson detailed decades ago that if Indigenous women's lives, needs and experiences were ever going to be valued, white feminists would need to let go of power and only then could feminist practice 'contribute to changing the racial order'.

The year Queensland decriminalised abortion the state's ombudsman found one in six Indigenous children did not have a birth certificate, which would potentially prevent them from enrolling in school, accessing government benefits or getting a driver's licence. In New South Wales, the legislative pushes to decriminalise abortion and make it more private were underway at the same time adoption without parental consent was legalised, despite the landmark 'Bringing Them Home' report released two decades earlier recommending that statutory adoption be a last resort for Aboriginal and Torres Strait Islander children. A 2020 report found 40 per cent of children in out-of-home care were Aboriginal, nearly ten times the rate of non-Indigenous children. The campaign to decriminalise abortion in the Northern Territory gained momentum in the year Australians watched horrifying footage of young people in the Don Dale Detention Centre outside Darwin being stripped down, physically held down, abused, hooded and bound in a manner the prime minister himself likened to Abu Ghraib and Guantanamo Bay. The following year, abortion was decriminalised in the region while a toothless Royal Commission into the Protection and Detention of Children in the Northern Territory failed to bring criminal charges against anyone responsible for the violations perpetrated against these children, and its recommendation to raise the age of criminal responsibility from ten to 12 is yet to be implemented. Data released the next year showed every single child in youth detention in the Northern Territory was Aboriginal.

These contrasts aren't about priorities – ideally, we would live in a country in which people have control over and safety within their own bodies and children are not criminalised, unsafe and removed from their families – but they tell us something about which community campaigns politicians and lawmakers will eventually respond to. They tell us when and for whom the patriarchy might bend. White middle-class feminists have long used the state to achieve safety and autonomy. As I write, there is momentum around criminalising coercive control in domestic relationships. As many abolitionist feminists have pointed out, these approaches, while intended to support survivors seeking justice, rely on a faith in policing and the criminal justice system that many victims can't afford to have. Almost 500 Indigenous people have died in custody, five in the month I write, in the 30 years since a Royal Commission into Aboriginal Deaths in Custody made a series of recommendations. Many of the suggestions are yet to be acted on while others were done so in a piecemeal way and in some cases only after years of campaigning and activism led by grieving families. 'Mass incarceration and criminalisation of Aboriginal people has been ongoing in this state since colonisation,' Dr Hannah McGlade addressed a Black Lives Matter rally in June 2020. 'There is racial profiling and discrimination at every stage of the criminal justice process.' A feminism that pushes towards greater engagement with any system of violence and discrimination is never going to bring the survivors of that violence and discrimination with it.

Gomeroi academic and author Amy Thunig felt undermined by medical professionals even as a teenager. When she was 16, all of her friends were going on the contraceptive pill so they could skip their periods and so she asked her doctor if she could do the same. He refused until she had done a pregnancy test even though she was not sexually active. 'Being made to do a pregnancy test in exchange for the script, even when I explained I had never had sex, made me feel frustrated and not believed,' she says. 'Not being heard within medical systems became an ongoing thing. It drains you of time, energy, everything. In my late 20s I developed a mix of pretty severe symptoms, but I ended up having to fight to access a pretty basic diagnosis . . . It always comes down to not being believed and having your physical pain treated as psychosomatic.' Amy was finally diagnosed with endometriosis and fibromyalgia when she was 32, even though she'd had years of pain so debilitating it made her vomit and had been hospitalised for anaemia from the heavy bleeding that accompanies endometriosis. 'After seeing white male doctor after white male doctor for three years and still having no diagnosis I said, "I'm so sick of seeing stale, pale and male, who can I see next?"' She sought out a female gynecologist. 'I will never forget that first appointment,' Amy says, her voice breaking. 'She looked at me and said, "I have been through all the notes on your file and I want to know if you've ever read them."' The doctor explained that the first specialist Amy had seen about her pain wrote down that she was just stressed and that her symptoms were psychological. The next specialist was going off these notes, as was the next one. After years of delay, Amy was booked in for surgery and the endometriosis tissue was lasered off. The gynecologist also referred her to a rheumatologist who diagnosed Amy with fibromyalgia.

Amy chose to start having children at 22 in part because Indigenous people have a lower life expectancy and she wanted her children to know their Elders. 'I wanted them to grow up with the strong Aboriginal people who raised me up, especially my Grandfather Malcolm,' she says. '[Parenting is] like a lot of things for Indigenous people – the violence and the rage is always going to be there in the systems we are forced to navigate but simultaneously there is great joy and great abundance in our community when it comes to support and love and guidance and I couldn't do anything without the support of my Elders and community.'

Amy also wanted to give herself time to build professional and financial stability, so by the time her children were school-aged she could give them more opportunities. 'It was a conscious choice to have my children young, and while I was studying, because I didn't have any generational wealth or access or anything to fall back on and I have been financially independent since I was 15,' she says. 'I knew that to build myself any stability or career and the kind of empowerment I knew I wanted long-term as a parent and a woman would take a long time.'

There is a low maternal mortality rate in Australia but Aboriginal and Torres Strait Islander mothers are more than twice as likely to die in association with pregnancy and childbirth. They are almost twice as likely as non-Indigenous mothers to have a baby with a low birth weight and they are less likely to attend an antenatal visit in the first trimester.

When Amy arrived at the hospital to give birth to her first child, she had already been labouring for two days but was ignored and dismissed by the staff. A midwife rebuked her for using a high-pitched voice during contractions and denied her access to the pain medication she requested, instead telling her to soften her shoulders and 'relax'. 'It was an ordeal, things only improved when I'd laboured for so long in hospital that there was a shift change and I got a new midwife. The trauma of that birth experience was so full-on that for three years, I said I wouldn't have any more children,' she says. 'I was so scared to be in that vulnerable state and to be completely not listened to, not supported and to have no control. It should have been a magical experience and it was traumatic.' For her second birth, Amy chose to birth at a different hospital, an additional 40 minute drive away, and paid for a birthing doula to be in the room – 'not because I wanted someone to rub my feet but I wanted a bulldog' to advocate for her.

I am suspicious of motherhood but few people would be suspicious of me as a mother. Not doctors, not police, not bystanders. In that way I have more freedom than many women. I still expect that motherhood would be laden with guilt and judgement but most likely from people I know, not institutions through which I need safety, justice, support or care.

For some women motherhood can be a shield, where for others, it is a target. In the wake of the Nice terror attacks in 2016, breakfast television host Sonia Kruger said that she would ban Muslim migration the following day if she had the power. After she was criticised, she tweeted that 'as a mother' she believed it was vital to be able to have these discussions without being labelled a racist. In our newsroom, 'as a mother' became a kind of cheeky shorthand for the ways in which usually rich, white women with platforms used the fact they had offspring to defend their bigotry. For white women, motherhood can come with an assumed valour, eliciting forgiveness and care.

The number of Indigenous children being removed and placed into child protection systems is still escalating, and the number of Indigenous children in out-of-home care is expected to double by 2029. Aboriginal and Torres Strait Islander children make up only 6 per cent of the child population in Australia but 37 per cent of the out-of-home care population. Amy refers to a tweet by an Indigenous journalist who, on her son's 18th birthday, announced that she was finally able to throw away the journals she'd kept since he was born detailing how she had cared for him in case anyone ever took him away.

Amy says the risk of a healthcare professional contacting child services makes every interaction with staff more stressful. 'It impacts everything. It impacts your autonomy as a parent.' Amy knows that refusing a treatment or wanting a second opinion can be taken as neglect. 'I tend to be over-the-top with being risk-averse because I am aware if my child has hurt themself and it turns out it's worse than it looks, I know how easy it would be to be labelled that negligent Aboriginal mother who didn't seek support, who wasn't looking after their child,' she says. 'There is so much less grace for Indigenous parents when it comes to how we treat our children and what we offer our children and what we see as an emergency and what we see as a bump or a scrape.' A healthcare worker threatened to contact child services when Amy did not take the immediate medical route they had suggested for her child. 'What was really frustrating about that was I was going to agree to it anyway,' she said. 'They were so ready and so quick to pull out that "you will do this" and "you will do this today" and "you will give your permission to this or I will contact Services and report" . . . I didn't even get to take a minute or ask questions about what the treatment looked like or what happens if we do, what happens if we do nothing, what are the risks, what are the possibilities. I didn't even get to have that conversation.'

Amy has driven the two hours each way to access specialist medical services in the city because she knows there are services nearby that are racially unsafe, which she acknowledges is a privilege. She recently took a risk on one of these public specialist services after assurance from her GP that she did not need to go private. 'The very first phone call with them was so violent and aggressive and when I said to them "thank you very much but I won't be using your service", they sent a letter to my GP alleging that I had decided to not have my child looked after at all and claiming that they had tried to refer me to private providers but that I had declined as I didn't want to pay for things, which wasn't true at all,' she says. 'I have the means to go elsewhere, and had been going elsewhere . . . [but] that is a privilege five years ago I wouldn't have been able to afford.'

The medical incarceration of Indigenous people has a long history. There were still forcibly removed Indigenous people detained in 'lock hospitals' in the early 70s, which, as Melissa Sweet, Kerry McCallum and Lynore Geia have pointed out, 'are archetypal examples of the role of healthcare professionals and systems in colonisation, contributing to intergenerational traumas'. As Vanamali Hermans writes, interrogating the governmentality of healthcare requires not just a biological but a social under-standing of the health impacts of the way marginalised bodies have to navigate the world. 'You need only ask any Blackfulla or disabled person in this country why we die younger or have poorer healthcare outcomes. It is not a question of our genes or response to healthcare systems, but of dispossession, ableism, racism and poverty,' Hermans writes. 'It is not the white, abled middle-class who die of chronic diseases in droves, or whose bodies bear the brutal-ity of state violence. Instead it is those of us continually marginalised who fill hospital beds.'

Medical institutions that might represent safety or support for non-Indigenous mothers are still sites of hyper-surveillance and racism for Amy. 'As a parent and as an Indigenous mother, I am constantly aware that they don't exist as a neutral system that you can access and that will always work for you,' she says. Amy sighs. 'It is always a risk. You're always walking that line of wanting to advocate for your child but also not wanting to be taken as an aggres-sive resistant parent.' The system is violent and it is not built for her, she says. 'We have made our best attempts to retrofit, to carve out some space, to make adjustments so you might be culturally understood and safe.'

Arrernte woman and midwife Cherisse Buzzacott makes space in her work for the safety and understanding that she was never afforded during a traumatic third pregnancy that resulted in her daughter being born at 21 weeks. Cherisse knew she was going into labour but no one was listening. Each medical professional she encountered was disbelieving of her pain, including a doctor who, when Cherisse pushed her hand away, asked for a note to be made: 'refusal to be examined'. Cherisse begged the midwife for a drink of water and the midwife told her to say please and thank you. 'I accepted this care and this attitude because I was vulnerable,' she wrote. 'She knew that I was a midwife, an English-speaking, university-educated Aboriginal woman, yet I was victimised. If this can happen to me, imagine the situation for those Aboriginal women without support, English as a second and third language, sitting in a white-walled room, thousands of kilometres away from community, culture, and strong birthing knowledge.' She wrote that she felt as if she might die.

I interviewed Cherisse in 2019 after research revealed that the model of maternal and infant care she had been running was successfully addressing the fact that Indigenous mothers were almost twice as likely to give birth to premature babies as non-Indigenous mothers. Birthing on country or birthing in community programs aim to bring cultural birthing traditions and community support to mainstream maternity services and, in some cases, make birthing in the community easier, sparing Indigenous women hundreds of kilometres of travel away from their support systems. Cherisse told me how the program had begun with yarning circles – consultations with local Aboriginal women, with Elders, with mothers, non-Indigenous health professionals working in maternity services, and other stakeholders. 'A lot of the women aren't birthing in their local communities, they're birthing in Canberra and Sydney and travelling a long way because the [local] hospitals are so culturally unsafe and they've suffered racism there,' she said. 'There were grandmothers who spoke about how they were treated really badly, and these women said, "this is healing for me even just talking about the possibility of an Aboriginal birth centre".'

The initiative was incredibly successful. It reduced the risk of a preterm birth – which can contribute to childhood disability, chronic illnesses and mortality – by almost half compared to hospital-based tertiary maternity services. Still, she said, they were struggling to secure more funding, particularly for an Aboriginal birthing centre. As Amy said, there are and have always been community-led solutions that are trying to build sanctuaries within an unsafe system but they are not always supported. These solutions are often led by Aboriginal women.

'We need programs initiated by us,' Cherisse wrote. 'Why shouldn't we have a right to say what happens to our bodies?'

Sexuality, pregnancy and motherhood are 'deeply racialised experiences', Caroline McFadden insists, and we should look at the privileges we have throughout them that rest on the disempowerment of other women. 'Those interconnections are not always pretty or palatable, but often laden with racism, colonialism, imperialism, and privilege,' she writes, proposing her own approach to begin asking questions which she calls critical white feminism. In the case of reproductive justice, this would mean we stop assuming our experiences are universal and common, stop pretending there is nothing to interrogate, encourage communication between women, help de-marginalise women of colour, secure racism as a priority issue, look back on what we have prioritised and ask which women it benefits, and include mothers and would-be mothers. 'A true self is not an isolated self that engages in self-reflection without cognition of others; instead, a true self interprets itself in relation to others by comparing and contrasting similarities and differences, not as a stimulant for fear and uncertainty, but as an act of human solidarity,' McFadden writes.

I want to reorient myself away from circumscribed victimhood and towards a collective responsibility. When you redefine reproductive oppression it allows you to reinterpret reproductive liberty as Dorothy E Roberts has. She writes that these rights have for too long been translated as negative – pushing against state interference rather than a positive right – getting the resources we all need to prevent pregnancy or have and parent a child. 'This view recognises the violation in a statute that bans a white, middle-class woman from taking the procreative option she wishes,' Roberts writes. 'But it disregards how poverty, racism, sexism, and other systems of power – often facilitated by government action – also impair many people's decisions about procreation.' A person's autonomy against oppressive government power is important, but as Roberts writes, 'liberalism has failed to deliver on its promise of freedom for all citizens'.

Any genuine effort to improve reproductive healthcare for everyone will value social justice as much as personal liberty. The right to parent your child without fear they will be taken away from you, the right to parent your child with enough support should you need it, the right to safe healthcare from pregnancy to birth and beyond. These rights must be as equally as important as the rights to prevent or terminate pregnancy.

Embedded within my misgivings about motherhood was an awareness of mother as a political category, even if it began as a blinkered fear of becoming politically irrelevant. I am asking how I accumulated the power I felt fearful of losing. I am asking how my body and those which I could help create move through the world. I am evaluating the organisations I encounter along the way, in my work, in my relations, in a potential pregnancy or parenthood. In critical white motherhood, we would be vigilant in asking and asking again where we assist, benefit from and partake in white supremacy.

The Most Important Job in the World

I know this will involve, as Erika Derkas writes, contesting 'unearned, stolen, socially constructed, and assumed privileges built off the lives of others'. We would ask questions about how our families are upholding structures of oppression or how we are helping to make them safer, how we are voting and participating in our communities, how we are redirecting our resources to communities where it is not appropriate for us to involve ourselves but to help them accommodate their most vulnerable, where we are living and sending our children to school, where we are donating and volunteering, what history we are teaching or not teaching our children and why, how we are paying the rent while living on stolen land. The violence, the suffering, the inequity any person suffers is real but for too long for white middle-class women our experiences of gender have been the main lens through which we are willing to understand and organise when it comes to family planning and parenting. The question of parenthood is a prompt to ask more questions about our politics. It is a chance to ask what we want to reproduce in ourselves and in the world we know it, whether or not we physically reproduce.

Shame and guilt can be paralysingly self-involved emotions but we can do better than acknowledging that our struggles are not as marginalised as those of other women.

Koa Beck writes that acknowledging privilege has become an avoidant transparency disclaimer for white feminists rather than what it should be – a 'perforation'. It should be painful. It should tear us open, open us up.

It should lay bare what the priorities, goals and strategies of 'personalised autonomy, individual wealth, perpetual self-optimization and supremacy' have actually done for other women. Understanding the smallness of our world should not make us retreat further into the confines of our experience; it should encourage us to learn the history, needs and struggles of people beyond it. This connection can mean stepping up, stepping back or stepping down. It can mean using resources to decentre yourself and demarginalise others. At the bare minimum it can mean being honest about the rationality of your own fear. Uncomfortably, for a group of women practiced at personalising before politicising growth, it can also mean understanding that progress will not be measured by your own individual experience of pregnancy, motherhood, healthcare and justice. 'The revolution will not be you alone, despite what white feminism has told you,' Beck writes. 'There is only the resistance movements that you will build with other people.'

4

Work

Love has always been a verb to me. It is something you do. An expression, an action, an exertion. I am a husk filled mostly with all I want to do for the people I love. It would be chic to quietly emanate love like moonlight – a coy glow settling on the rooftops of your dearest as they fall asleep, a comforting presence they know to be there if they look for it out the window. But my love is hot and garish like sunlight – I want to help you photosynthesise, I want to dry your laundry, I want my kisses to leave constellations of freckles across your cheeks. I can't stay still long enough to suspend myself in love as a noun – a state, a feeling, a passive reality, a fact once established, never tested, a framed photograph collecting dust on a mantelpiece.

When I learned about love languages, I felt for the first time fluent in something – speaking with my time, words, body, energy, and trinkets – and simultaneously nervous that my love might seem like a performance. But the displaying

133

is the loving. And I love loving. Without the work, the love remains a presumption, distant, rarely visited, hanging silently above us in the night sky.

The problem with accepting labour as a function of love is that it is a prerequisite for buying into most exploitative folklore about both motherhood and paid employment. The idea that unpaid domestic labour and caring work isn't work at all, it is love and so need not be recognised or compensated, is ancient propaganda while the notion that you must 'do what you love' has become a misleading ethos for working millennials. The problem with interrogating a motherhood built on the myth of love as labour or questioning a paid job that requires labour as love is that it complicates the question of what to devote yourself to and where you might find meaning in your life. The problem with finding a ready answer for a readily asked question – *if not kids, then what?* – is that I am running out of time.

A career felt like a complete answer to me until it didn't. A woman whose entire life revolved around her job was enviable until she wasn't. Yet, even if it was financially viable, I can't imagine ever completely abandoning paid employment.

People have always been aware of how parenthood would interrupt their career trajectory and for those who have invested their selfhood into their jobs, as many of us have, a child threatens to disrupt not just our earning capacity but our identity. Parental leave isn't only a drop in hours but a voluntary, even if often temporary, desertion of a central place of meaning-making. Now I find myself considering how dramatically my love and labour would be divided in parenthood and all that I would need to abandon about how I value myself and how I would expect others to, particularly those holding political and industrial power. I now need to consider for whom I toil – work, family, both, neither – and how I would do so. The only things more tedious than conversations about 'having it all' are the conditions that necessitate them. Stubborn statistics show women continue to arrive home from full-time work to perform a second shift of unpaid labour – globally, women and girls still perform $10.8 trillion worth of unpaid labour every year. The latest census found Australian men are working an average of 39 hours per week while women are working an average of 30 paid hours per week but were twice as likely as men to do more than 15 hours of additional domestic work. Most workplaces are still fundamentally not set up to support primary carers. We know one in two mothers and one in four fathers in Australia have reported experiencing discrimination in the workplace at some point during pregnancy, parental leave or on their return to work. We know mothers who went back to work before they were ready to, anxious about the growing gap in their resume. We know mothers who retired with half as much superannuation as their partners. We know working mothers who said, as did the research, that home-schooling fell to them during the pandemic. We know mothers who felt self-conscious about their choice to have kids ahead of their careers. 'We're contemptuous of "lazy" poor mothers. We're contemptuous of "distracted" working mothers. We're contemptuous of "selfish" rich mothers,' Kim Brooks writes. 'We're contemptuous of mothers who have no choice but to work, but also of mothers who don't need to work and still fail to fulfil an impossible ideal of selfless motherhood.' To consider how you might ration your love and labour for the rest of your life is to consider how you might be perceived for that allocation.

A friend with a toddler is the first and, she believes, the last, to have a child in her friendship group as her peers are prioritising their careers. 'I feel like a bumpkin sometimes,' she admits. My instinct is to remind her how amazing she is at her job, how well-read she is, how her career will progress as theirs have once her kid is older and she is back at work, but I stop myself. She shouldn't have to feel valued as a paid worker while her shift as an unpaid worker never ends. She is a working mother as all mothers are. The next time we speak, she is exhausted because her kid hasn't been sleeping and she feels like she can't ask more care of her partner, who is still working full-time. He says he will 'take' the kid for a few hours, that he will 'mind' him. I tell her this is just parenting. Later she says, 'Sometimes I just think "what has feminism done for me lately?"'

I am in the generation of goal-setting, opportunity-seizing, yes-saying professionally starving women who, as Lisa Miller writes, are now realising they have been sold another 'bullshit promise' – that the workplace would provide total fulfilment as their mothers and grandmothers were promised the home would. 'The men in charge are still in charge,' she writes. 'It is impossible for women to continue to have faith in a vision of their own empowerment, when that empowerment is, in fact, a pose.' Don't turn to the workplace as previous generations of women were encouraged to turn to their husbands – to answer the big questions about your life, Miller implores.

My newfound disillusionment with a life built only around a career has not made a life structured around a child more appealing. 'The days with the baby felt long but there was nothing expansive about them,' Jenny Offill writes. 'Caring for [my baby] required me to repeat a series of tasks that had the peculiar quality of seeming both urgent and tedious.' My working life has been nothing if not a series of urgent and tedious tasks – rushing to report on breaking news, transcribing hours of interviews, jumping in a cab to a press conference, making fruitless inquiry after fruitless inquiry, fact checking once, twice, thrice – and yet it is waged, it is visible, and it is valorised because historically it has been done by men.

I was indeed sold a bullshit promise and yet at least in full-time work without children, I have some predictability, the promise of a linear path to something that looks like success, a series of problems to be solved with resources to solve them and little treats when I do so, some respect within the places I've learned to seek it.

When I was a cadet journalist, a man who held a senior columnist position at the newspaper politely approached me to talk about a then topical debate on whether politicians should be allowed to breastfeed at work. 'How is that any different from a male politician asking to masturbate in the chamber?' he asked in complete seriousness. I didn't know how to respond to someone who thought feeding a child should be as private an act as sexual gratification. I understood then that the sight of employed women was less offensive to some men than having to witness the obscenity, the sheer work of mothering.

I am considering motherhood after spending a decade committed to the idea that women find their freedom in the workplace, glamorising what is paid and sympathising with or ignoring what is not. I am reconsidering where employment belongs in a life well lived and how I came to understand it as the foundation. I have inconveniently stopped believing in many of the fairy tales that informed my plans for where I would find meaning in my life just as my career ascends and my fertility declines.

For any potential parent there are practical negotiations to be made with partners, employers and themselves about the division of paid and unpaid labour in households likely dependent on two incomes. Even for people whose sense of self is healthily unattached from the demands of their job, all of us poised on the threshold of this decision have questions to answer about work and family, the answers to which will follow us into parenthood, should we choose it.

*

Before the ambivalence there was something that felt like ambition. I realised it was a scam to pretend producing progeny wasn't actual work long before I understood the grift of profit-producing as progress. The women in my family had been homemakers and I resented the notion that I needed to construct my identity in the home because of my gender. This was fostered by the first kind of feminism I was exposed to. It was a hunger embodied by the childfree characters, though few and far between, I saw represented on television – the hedonistic Samantha Jones, the imperfect Elaine Benes, the tragic Liz Lemon, the ambitious Jessica Pearson and of course the impervious Cristina Yang – 'I choose medicine, I choose me, I choose that over the remote possibility that I might one day regret not having a child'. I allowed motherhood and its domestic labour to be degraded by the logic of a corporate feminism which fetishised the enlightening, empowering and stimulating potential of paid work. Alicia Florrick, the attorney in *The Good Wife*, smiles as her son says, 'Sometimes I think of you as Mom, and other times just as this interesting person who lives in our house.' There was a time when it would have been a status symbol for a woman not to have to work but now that the workplace is understood as a site of intellectual growth and weight, camaraderie and creativity, paid employment is a sign you have made it. I wanted to be the interesting person who lived in the house, before I considered populating it with children.

Mainstream feminism feels increasingly out of step with social ideals of equality, rights and justice and, as Catherine

139

Rottenberg points out, more often compatible with political and economic agendas of free-market capitalism, consumerism and privatisation. When I began university, feminism was not only socially acceptable but marketable. This was radical for an 18-year-old who wasn't raised a feminist. I felt part of something that validated my experiences of womanhood so far. It was learning what consent was and wasn't, it was body positivity on Instagram, it was girls in my uni tutorials growing their underarm hair, it was encountering intersectionality and privilege and then failing to do anything meaningful with it, it was realising there was a gender pay gap, it was freeing your nipples, it was fugly 'fuck the patriarchy' tote bags and enamel pins, it was wanting to be a #girlboss in the #workplace, it was a messy introduction to the most self-interested and least self-aware form of neoliberal white feminism you could imagine.

I began a cadetship at a newspaper staffed mostly by greying conservative men. I felt completely out of my depth and I was grateful that there was a journalist looking out for me. She didn't have children but she had a lot of front-page stories. She gave me a copy of Sheryl Sandberg's *Lean In* to help me survive. I was at an age where a lot of my friends were in and out of relationships with men who behaved appallingly and then responded to their girlfriend's distress by telling her things she could alter about herself if she wanted the relationship to work. It was her reaction to his behaviour that was disrupting the relationship. That's how I felt reading *Lean In*. The conditions need not change; I just had to become less sensitive to them. 'We can reignite the revolution by internalising the revolution,' Sandberg told me. Find a way to make sure you were in an office higher up in the building but don't damage any infrastructure on the way up.

It was a hierarchical workplace where stress pressed downwards, hard, and I was at the very bottom and so was told 'failure is not an option', 'if you don't find the right case study today, we don't have a front page' and 'don't take a sick day again – if your leg falls off, bring it in with you'. The culture of bullying, the sexism and harassment, the glee taken in watching newcomers learn by suffering – it was my problem, and I was ready to be a good feminist and turn it all inwards, at least for long enough, I told myself, to get a job at a publication where I could do work that felt meaningful. I saw the advancement of my own career as liberation from the expectations of womanhood. All of this work, even in my self-interest, could be a feminist act. If I worked hard enough, if I made myself useful enough, if I mimicked men in the workplace for long enough, I would eventually have the freedom they did to pursue the stories I wanted to.

This attitude didn't last long. One day I was out on a job with a middle-aged straight-talking photographer I looked up to. Over the preceding weeks we had been sent out to pursue several impossible stories during which the chief-of-staff or editor would call almost hourly to gruffly ask whether we'd been successful yet in securing a front-page photo.

It was jarring to hear her shift from her natural bluntness to an almost slavish tone as she responded to the hounding requests of men we'd usually spent all day slandering. At that time newspapers had all but scrapped their photography departments and this freelancer was on a random roster sometimes decided on the day. As we drove to the next location I told her it was unreasonable that someone with her experience and talent should have to be routinely spoken to like that. I think I secretly wanted her to talk back, to stop apologising and start asserting her needs as a man would, as Sheryl Sandberg might. As she hauled her big clunky van around the corner, her hands pulling at the wheel, she said, 'Gina, in this business, a lot of the time you've just gotta bend over, grab your ankles and take it.' I was shocked, not by the lewdness of the metaphor but by the honest resignation, the antithesis of putting your hand up and asking for a seat at the table. This photographer was telling me how to survive and, in the end, she was right – I found far less friction bending over than leaning in.

I left the newspaper and fell in love with my new job, reporting primarily on sexual and reproductive rights for *BuzzFeed News*. I was writing about something so sparsely covered in Australia that I was able to break new ground each week with ongoing legislative pushes and political debates on abortion that kept the momentum going. I had the kind of freedom and autonomy unheard of for reporters my age and I was working with a team of people who felt more like friends than colleagues. The difficult and boring moments in the job were irrelevant in between the genuine fulfilment. I had no interest in climbing an editorial ladder. I didn't need career progression, I had meaning. I had arrived at where I wanted to stay. Our 9 am news meeting was my favourite part of the day, when I got to sit and listen to talented smart people pitch stories that I cared about – revealing the unending brutality of Australia's offshore and onshore detention regime, covering fascinating court cases and exposing how climate denialists, anti-vaxxers and white supremacists were using social media to network and spread misinformation. Our colleagues abroad were dropping high-profile global investigations into fraud, corruption, sexual assault and harassment, torture and murder, as well as the US government and the president's finances. I was a person who used the phrase 'dream job'. The question of motherhood was answered. I wanted only to bear fruit in service of journalism. I loved my editors, I loved my readers, I loved my interviewees, I loved my work. I was enamoured in a way that was so consuming it is embarrassing now. 'If caring work is familial love, based in the all-sacrificing love of the mother, creative work is romantic love, based in a different kind of self-sacrifice and voluntary commitment that is expected, on some level, to love you back,' labour journalist Sarah Jaffe writes. 'Yet work never, ever loves you back.'

In mid-2020 our entire reporting team was laid off as the economic impact rippled through the already contracting news media industry. I had been working seven years full-time and in the wake of my redundancy, I felt incapable of saying no to any freelance opportunity and found myself working most days to meet competing deadlines. I was anxious to make rent but above all, I knew I was frantically trying to maintain my identity as a journalist. I just wanted to keep doing what I loved.

'Where on earth did you get this Protestant work ethic?' my mother's bemused voice echoed down the phone line. '*Actually, it is Catholic guilt, and I got it from you*,' I thought to myself bitterly. This was untrue. I had not inherited my inability to extricate my identity and sense of self-worth from my job from my mother, who had been a schoolteacher for most of my life and had always worked to live, not lived to work.

Work has become if not the one, then certainly a central place of meaning-making for many people my age. Even those who loathe their employment feel somewhat defined by it and often complain not just of the long hours, shitty pay and lack of security but also of the monotony, the futility and lack of creativity required. Eda Gunaydin writes that it is a 'millennial rite of passage' to convert our passions into jobs or at least side hustles. 'The advice to Westerners, and middle or upper-middle classes, is that we should follow our bliss, start businesses that mEaN SoMeThInG to us or – if we are employed in impersonal work – that we personalise it: invest real emotions, or our individual flair,' she writes. The cult of productivity cares not for hobbies, so you should either pursue meaning by monetising your hobby or else find a way to make your job feel as personal as your hobby.

The neoliberal project has moved beyond promoting the joy that can be found in the material benefits of capitalism to reimagining work as 'a source of joy in and of itself', says Miya Tokumitsu. 'Seductive slogans about work as self-actualisation and images of blissful labour are ubiquitous,' she writes. The virtue in work changed from suffering to pleasure with the Baby Boomer generation, Tokumitsu claims, when a 'culture of self' arose and people were thinking more about their own improvement and fulfilment. This 'do what you love' (DWYL) rhetoric has helped sell overwork and sleep deprivation as fulfilling, she says. It has helped rebrand exhaustion as a status symbol that tells the world that you are needed, you are skilled, and you are special. The devotion must be unwavering. 'After all, ideal love is nothing if not constant,' Tokumitsu writes.

For a few years, I felt I was a journalist before I was anything else. I could not see a future in which it wasn't the main source of connection, community and fulfilment in my life. It was where I felt I offered the most value to the world. It was where I felt useful, smart, capable, creative, impactful and resilient. It was only when I became less naive about the limits of journalism, and by that I mean less naive about the limits of truth, that I began seeking out other ways to become a more useful citizen, strategising about where I put my time and money and why. My redundancy story wasn't special – at least 150 newsrooms in Australia shut during 2020 and the same week I was laid off, a Pulitzer Prize winner was put on unpaid furlough – and yet it felt personal. I hadn't just lost a job, I'd lost what I thought made me, me. I felt worth less without it.

The chance to be consumed by and compensated for this kind of work is of course attainable to very few people. 'Polite society may prefer to pretend otherwise, but the kind of jobs that provide public visibility, ready-made identities, and the promise of self-fulfilment are strictly cordoned off by class boundaries,' Tokumitsu writes. 'DWYL provides cover for beguiling ourselves that work and class float free from each other, that the work one does is a function of personal choice rather than class membership and that class membership is a function of nebulous other facts, often implying strength (or frailty) or moral character.' Those who *choose* to overwork are lauded and those who *have* to overwork or who want adequate hours to get by are ignored.

However, it is wrong to assume the desire for meaningful work is always the product of affluence, that once we have attained our physical and economic security, we are able to reach up the shelves of Maslow's hierarchy of human needs, fumbling around for love and belonging, esteem and self-actualisation in our employment. But as Jamie McCallum writes, it is the opposite. Workers' demands for edifying work emerged from the boring monotony of factory work in the 70s and gained momentum as the economic rewards for work declined. This isn't just a preference – some people caring more about social or emotional benefits than monetary ones – but a seismic societal shift, a reconstruction of our 'cultural scaffolding' in which meaning becomes supplementary rather than complementary to the wages and benefits of a work package, McCallum says. 'The worse work gets and the less we are paid to do it, the more meaningful we are told it should be.' I highlight the passage and make a note: *like motherhood?*

Everything we used to value outside of paid employment has been braided into it and companies are investing in company 'culture' faster than you can say 'minimum wage'. I loved it. For four years I believed work was a place I would always be excited to go to and that there were decades of fun and novelty to come. I didn't care about the job's most alienating attributes, I didn't need wage growth – I had subsidised exercise classes, work drinks, catered lunch twice a week, free avocado toast on Fridays, unlimited protein balls and a kombucha machine. Working for an organisation headquartered in the United States felt like a preview into where all employers who were investing heavily in non-monetary perks were headed. In December, the chief executive would wear a tacky Christmas jumper and reveal what this year's present would be. One year, it was wireless headphones. We had a 'culture club' – in lieu of proper HR – to ensure we had fun ways to recognise people's work and events to look forward to. They once gave us a massage voucher to apologise for how long it had taken to subsidise private health insurance, a perk I didn't use because, and I'm not sure if they were aware of this, we have universal healthcare in Australia.

When I spent a week working from my former employer's New York office, I sat at my desk, enjoying the free bagels and unlimited complimentary froyo and, for the first time in my life, I felt like a misanthrope. I peered around, quietly marvelling at the unceasing extraversion, the high-fiving, the unrelenting niceness to each other, someone chirping, 'neat!' and another, 'awesome!', one person telling another they'd love to take them bouldering. They still wore the grinning cynicism reporters all don to cope in a job that requires you to consume news all day but it couldn't compete with this springy camaraderie that felt foreign, as it didn't seem to be built on a foundation of making fun of each other.

Jasmine, an Australian working for Seattle-based tech company Amazon, laughs knowingly. 'I am so careful at work about what I joke about and I really have to tone down my sarcasm,' she says.

It is not just the earnestness but the blinkered emphasis on work that Jasmine finds bewildering. 'It is this American psyche of your purpose in life being linked to work,' she says. Jasmine wholeheartedly bought into it for 18 months until she was so burned out, she had to acknowledge her values just didn't align with the premise. 'You do feel a sense of achievement and I get excited about work and the stuff we do at scale but we have these tag lines like "work hard, have fun, make history" and I have my fun in other ways,' she says. 'Work isn't the highlight of my year when I look back.' Jasmine explained a common practice where managers tell people they are earmarked for a promotion but wait a year to give it to them. 'It drives people to work extra hard for a long period of time and then they eventually get rewarded for it.'

Amazon's owner Jeff Bezos calls the hard work a 'bias for action' but former employees have described it as 'a drug that we could get self-worth from'. As one of the company's HR goals declares: 'Employees come to Amazon to do meaningful work.'

Jasmine works hard and long hours but now stops once she has closed her laptop for the day. 'I don't feel guilt,' she says.

When a woman in her team seemed to be having a bad day and eventually admitted she was struggling to steady herself during the hormonal fluctuations that accompany the weeks of injections needed for egg retrieval, Jasmine learned that Amazon pays for egg freezing as a company benefit. In Australia, egg freezing costs around AUD\$7,000 per cycle and six months storage. Jasmine knew she wanted children one day but hadn't met the right person. For a few weeks, she injected herself twice a day with a syringe to stimulate her hormones, her eggs were then collected and they are now sitting in a freezer somewhere in Seattle. 'I was surprised at how much of a difference it made to how I was feeling,' Jasmine says. 'I felt free.' She finally feels like she can take her time with dating and find someone who she is compatible with long-term instead of settling for a partner who wasn't right for her. 'That would be a far worse outcome than not having a family.'

The rise of corporate egg-freezing subsidies – nearly one in five major US firms offer it – points to the fact that companies would rather buy more time with an unencumbered worker instead of investing in a workplace that might better suit mothers or others with caring commitments. A 2021 study found 42 per cent of Australian women were receptive to egg-freezing as a job benefit while 27 per cent of those surveyed were opposed to the idea, some saying it would pressure them to delay childbearing and exacerbate existing inequities in accessing assisted reproductive technologies. Jasmine says she feels like she has cheated the system and used her privilege to buy time others can't afford. But, as with all company benefits, they primarily benefit the company. 'In the short-term, they will get a lot more out of me because I will remain unmarried without children,' she says. '[Meanwhile] I like having this insurance policy because my fertility window is closing and I now have the freedom to take my time on this choice.' Amazon pays for the egg storage as long as she is an employee. I thought about Jack Donaghy, the comically cold-blooded executive on *30 Rock*, saying, 'Our healthcare costs are way down since we started putting something in the coffee to keep women from getting pregnant.'

In 2019, almost 2,000 of Amazon's working mothers, who called themselves The Momazonians, claimed the company discriminated against parents, particularly mothers, calling for Amazon to provide back-up childcare options so they could meet their work demands. It was only temporarily granted during the pandemic.

The Most Important Job in the World

Jasmine says one of her managers, a mother and primary caregiver of two children aged under five, was working more than full-time, sending emails in the early morning and late at night. 'One time I got a call from her and she said, "I'm just in the bathroom hiding from my children,"' Jasmine remembers. 'And I just said, "This call isn't that important."'

Jasmine's future options seem to be to delay parenthood supported by the company, balance parenthood with very little support from the company or become a mother and leave the company for somewhere that is more amenable to parenthood, as she plans to. 'No career ambition is worth sacrificing myself and my family not being able to see me.'

Time with family is compromised by the boundless nature of work as we now know it, while progression in the workplace is hindered by having anyone to care for but yourself.

It didn't have to be this way. In the 1970s in Padua, Italy, a radical campaign refused to put the workplace over the home as the most important site of women's liberation. Wages for Housework began drawing attention to the unpaid work women were doing – cooking, cleaning, rearing children, caring for the elderly – that kept paid workers fed and clothed. These physical, repetitive, skilled vital tasks were made visible not as acts of devotion but for what they were: labour. The movement's pamphlet, authored by Silvia Federici, 'Wages Against Housework'

(1975) opens: 'They say it is love. We say it is unwaged work.' She challenged the notion that housework was an aspiration 'coming from the depth of [their] female character', an innately womanly desire. 'Capital had to convince us that it is a natural, unavoidable and even fulfilling activity to make us accept our unwaged work,' it read. Nurturing is natural, housework is inevitable, mothering is purpose. On some of the pamphlets, an exhausted mother steadies herself with a broom as a flock of children tug at her skirt. In her other hand, she holds a wad of cash. The dollar sign is a tiny scribble but it makes the image feel radical even almost half a century later. The crass audacity to put a price on something you have been socialised to believe is as fulfilling as it is fated.

You only have to look at the wages of childcare workers, teachers and aged care workers to see how this lingering presumption complements a 'do what you love' ethos to devalue work that is traditionally gendered female. Care work in the home has been denigrated for so long that it still fails to be compensated fairly outside of it. Wages for Housework made exploitation a starting point. It was not an attempt to degrade or institutionalise love, nor an attempt to make husbands pay their housewives salaries; it was an attempt to dismantle the default inequitable organisation of the home by demanding wages. It was not discouraging women seeking work outside the home but sought to ensure they did so not out of desperation for a skerrick of financial independence but with genuine agency and autonomy. As Federici wrote, contraceptives are 'the only true labour-saving devices' – how else to seize the means of (re)production? 'No one's work will be done until the work of being a woman with no money is undone,' the 'Black Women for Wages for Housework Bulletin' of Autumn 1977 reads. These campaigners warned with eerie prescience that the first site of resistance should not be the workplace but the home. Paid employment was not going to free anyone until the enormous problem of unpaid work was dealt with. Neither the family nor the firm was going to liberate women. 'They wanted, instead, time for themselves, freedom to discover what love and sexuality might look like outside of relations of power and labour,' Jaffe observes of Federici and her peers. Women were entering the workforce as unions were losing power and employment became more precarious, or 'at the moment in which the roof of the factory was falling down' as Federici puts it. 'Women were expected to pick up the slack by taking up paid work while not reducing the amount of work they did in the home,' Jaffe writes. 'The new social conservatives, hand in hand with the ascendant neoliberals, aimed to reinforce the traditional nuclear family at the same time as policies were being put in place to wring more work out of everyone, reinstituting the Protestant work ethic by law if not by choice.'

Just as many of the material benefits of work are being supplemented by meaning, material benefits can be withheld if assigned 'meaning' is not fulfilled. On the day I write this, our government has announced it will extend a punitive scheme mostly targeting low-income single mothers with children under six. The program, ParentsNext, was condemned by our Human Rights Commission for being 'manifestly inconsistent' with our human rights obligations, as it docked welfare payments for parents who failed to attend 'story time' sessions and demanded domestic violence survivors retell their stories with their children present to keep payments.

'It should come as no surprise that, just as the scrutiny of mothers reaches new heights, the welfare nets that once provided material support for families are assiduously dismantled,' Camilla Nelson and Rachel Robertson write. 'What the scrutiny of mothers conceals is the reality of a world in which every woman is defined through the ideal of maternal care work, regardless of whether she is – or even wants to be – a mother.' Nelson and Robertson argue that blaming mothers for social ills makes inequality a matter of individual will and allows real material causes like poverty to go unaddressed. As Anwen Crawford has written, the financial hardship created by a disciplinary conception of welfare 'as the last resort of the least deserving' exacerbates gender inequality for single mothers. 'How, as a society, should we recognise and compensate for the labour of child-rearing and domestic work, which has almost always gone unpaid?' she writes. 'Is full-time wage labour the only means of measuring social contribution that we are prepared to endorse?'

Parenthood can sometimes feel like a path we are supposed to consider if we have cleared some undefined state of financial stability. We might not expect other people to do so – I don't judge my parents for having a child as penniless teenagers – but it is a standard I know many of us hold ourselves to. The notion that we should delay falling pregnant until we don't need welfare, have a stable career or adequate savings is, as Connor Kilpatrick points out, just the inverse of previous commands for women to stay at home and procreate. Both, he writes, ask women to defer to something beyond their desires. 'How can we ever win a program that socialises the costs of bringing children into the world if so many liberals still see the desire to have kids as something like a timeshare in Vegas – a costly, foolish, and tacky investment mostly for the rubes?' Kilpatrick writes. There is a personal and political cost to deciding parenthood is an indulgence.

I am trying to understand the obstacles faced along a single route to civic worth that leads out of the home and through the workplace. I see clearly now how equating my paid labour with my own value in society was not just foolish but in direct opposition with how I value other people. It does not square with how I value the time and effort of my brother, an unemployed person living in social housing, nor how I value my mother's domestic care on the days she wasn't teaching. Any progress, particularly for women, that confines itself to the workplace feels to me now not just incomplete but exclusionary. In overvaluing paid employment, we devalue what is underpaid or unpaid and allow the state to continue shafting the burdens of social reproduction on to families.

Just as the emphasis on all the rewarding but priceless qualities of care distract from the fight to make parenting affordable, an obsession with the noneconomic benefits of hard labour slows the fight for more good jobs – ones that might even feel compatible with parenthood. Even before the pandemic hit, wage growth had fallen short of the government's official forecasts for eight consecutive federal budgets and business elites blamed this on a lack of productivity. Our own prime minister said, 'Once you see that sustained productivity and that sustained profit, then that should flow through to wages.' As though if the average worker was producing a little more, they would be paid a little more, as though the lack of real wage increases has nothing to do with employers holding the balance of industrial power, as though profits had always trickled down to workers' pay packets in the most productive of our industries, as though bosses are loving parents, stuffing each of their children's Christmas stockings with extra treats at the end of a fruitful year. Workplaces aren't family units but in writing her book *Work Won't Love You Back*, Sarah Jaffe says she came across workers who told her their bosses defined them as such. 'With little time for a personal life anyway, we are even more likely to try to make work more pleasurable, even to seek in it a replacement for the love we lack elsewhere,' Jaffe writes. I invested my love and care into my team as though it was a family but ultimately, it was the union that exemplified what family means to me – a bunch of people who keep in irregular contact but sometimes show up for each other in a crisis. My mum turning up at midnight to collect me and my suitcase after an ugly breakup. It was the union who checked in, who answered my questions, who helped me understand my rights and made sure I wasn't screwed over with my severance package. This family should be bound by loyal ties that allow for collective imagination and action, not just reaction. A weaker workers' rights movement means there is less of a counterweight to business to fight for good conditions just when a generation of potential parents might need it most.

The question of having both children and a full-time career is fraught, not only because it is hard to imagine love divided but because the problem of unpaid labour can be solved for some via delegation. Households now usually rely on two incomes and with little time for housework and child-rearing, having it all seems a feat only possible if you have a partner who is a primary carer or if you are earning enough to outsource some domestic tasks. I have watched older women I know, particularly those without extended family networks like myself, give up on begging their husbands to contribute equally at home and instead hire babysitters, nannies and cleaners so they can keep their careers. Domestic workers, as Koa Beck writes, are essential to white feminists' 'self-interested and often capitalistic, ascension to gender equality – either within their homes, their workplaces or within their own families'. In this way, a whole cohort of women is in fact getting a wage for housework – not to tend to her own family but to take on the load of more highly paid white-collar workers. As Kimberly Seals Allers writes, the labour of some women is used to allow other women to pursue their corporate and civic dreams. The conversation about work-life balance often ignores the 'simple economics' of how we ended up here – 'White women had money but wanted more time. Black and brown women needed more money.' As Angela Davis wrote in 1981, 'women of colour – and especially Black women – have been receiving wages for housework for untold decades'. And yet, as she points out, we have been reticent about the fact that our ability to unmoor ourselves from the home has relied on this labour. A #girlboss narrative relies on a single heroine.

As Catherine Rottenberg points out, this situation only further solidifies market rationality while also 'creating new and reinforcing old class-based and racialised gender stratification'. The endgame, as Rottenberg sees it, will be a total economisation of reproduction. 'Once certain women are able to freeze their eggs successfully, rent a womb, as well as hire various caregivers, new and intensified forms of racialised and classed gender exploitation will occur,' she writes. 'Indeed, this trajectory of powerful women is bound to produce new populations of dispensable "service" providers, the vast majority of whom will be women.' I don't think Rottenberg is diminishing the place of assisted reproductive technology or surrogacy in many families but highlighting that neoliberal feminism does not service all women. As Kim Brooks writes, equality won't come from women foisting their exploitation onto less privileged women. Instead, she calls for women to collectively say: 'From now on, they have to pay us, because as women we do not guarantee anything any longer.' What kind of work-life balance relies on maintaining the invisible, devalued, and gendered nature of reproduction and care work? One that seems unsustainable for everyone involved.

Emma Goldman, an anarchist imprisoned in 1893 for inciting a riot with a speech to unemployed workers and later for disseminating birth control information, wrote of the 'narrowness' of the existing conception of woman's independence and emancipation. 'The dread of love for a man who is not her social equal; the fear that love will rob her of her freedom and independence; the horror that love or the joy of motherhood will only hinder her in the full exercise of her profession,' Goldman wrote. 'All these together make of the emancipated modern woman a compulsory vestal, before whom life, with its great clarifying sorrows and its deep, entrancing joys, rolls on without touching or gripping her soul.' A century later, this conception prevails. I find myself unmoored, soul untouched nor gripped, between the work of mothering and the work of reporting, a binary that says either, or, both, but never neither. How long left do I have to consider a life in which the most important thing isn't a job nor parenting but something else entirely? What is the sum that accounts for the labour I want to give my friends, my community, myself? How can I make space for that calculus and still pay rent? 'How do I create a fulfilling life for myself that isn't only work-focused?' a childless friend asks. 'What if you're not a careerist?'

Matresence, the anthropological concept which describes the identity transformation involved in becoming a mother, captures the friction between fantasy and reality, the guilt and the shame, the way you were mothered and the way you want to mother and the ambivalence, writes psychologist Dr Alexandra Sacks. 'Even those who don't experience [postpartum depression] are undergoing a significant transformation,' Sacks notes. I read about how slowly scholarship on mothers and their subjectivity has developed but I find writing on whatever the opposite of matresence is sparser still. I read about people who tried but could not have the family they wanted, those who devoted themselves to a job or cause, but find little on those who never wanted. I can't find a template for an ambivalent woman.

I call Judy, a family friend. I was obsessed with her as a child because she was a glamorous architect who toasted nuts before she put them on salads and had dinner parties with friends who stayed for days. She painted flowers and was the only adult I knew in a physically affectionate relationship. I idolised her because she did not have her own children. I could see how she had the luxury to tend to many things I imagined my mum might have time for if she didn't have four kids. Her partner was the first man his age I had encountered who was not in some way demented by the model of masculinity he had grown up with. He was gentle, affectionate, expressive, creative and not self-conscious about these facts. Now in their 70s, Judy confirms their life is as rich as I fantasised. As a child I thought she was a woman who chose architecture over children but I see now she chose many things instead. She is surrounded by friends, their children, their grandchildren. She still travels, she still paints. She is still deeply in love with her partner of four decades. Together they built the beautiful life they wanted. I didn't expect Judy to admit that underneath their decision not to have children, which was made many times, was a lot of fear. The financial cost of children, the toll it might take on their relationship, but specifically, the lack of control over who her children might be and the bad choices they might make. She lists parents and grandparents she knows whose children's decisions have caused them grief.

'The risk is just enormous,' she cackles. 'Maybe I'm a coward.'

How does categorically deciding you will not have children and then experiencing not having children transform you? Are the tensions the same? Who would I be without children? Who would I be without children and a career? Why does it still feel radical to admit I might want a life in which I am not preoccupied by either? I entertain notions of being an especially involved community member, an unbelievable cook, a more present auntie, a better friend to more people, enviably fit, the most well-read and well-travelled person you've ever met. In every scenario, I see myself endlessly producing. How would I protect any of these pursuits from the cult of productivity? 'In a situation where every waking moment has become the time in which we make our living . . . time becomes an economic resource that we can no longer justify spending on "nothing",' writes Jenny Odell. Is my disenchantment with the prospect of motherhood instead of, or, worse, alongside another four decades of journalism just early fatigue with the compulsion to prove I am devoted to doing *something*?

I had never considered I might not be consumed by something; for the first time I pictured myself consuming. I might want to sleep in, to stay at the pub for a few more, to miss both the sunrise and the sunset devouring two books per year that I'd never post a picture of, to enjoy more of my partner, to go for long walks, steps uncounted, to watch movies that won't make me a better person, to never grow a vegetable, to be free any night you are, to stay in the bath for longer and listen to my podcasts about D-grade celebrities. I might want to do this more often for the rest of my life. Even typing it out, my fingers feel sticky with something indulgent. But what if more idleness isn't self-interest but survival? What if from the ashes of the girlboss rises what Gabrielle Moss calls the girlloser? A feminism that doesn't see unorganised people as 'deadweight', that doesn't confuse 'focus, ambition and organisation with a celebration of womanhood', that doesn't instruct us to be 'painfully responsible', that doesn't paste hard worker over mother as the complete female identity. 'Everything is chaos, and being a boss can't protect you,' she writes. 'So you might as well give being a loser a shot.' If respite is not defeat and rest is not death and being average at something is permissible, the choices we make in an imperfect structure feel a little lighter.

After taking my job very seriously I was, ironically, made redundant by the very publisher of Anne Helen Petersen's ultra-viral essay about the burnout generation. Millions of millennials shared the article which summarised their situation – a generation with less savings, more debt, waning union protection and who couldn't take stable employment at the same company for granted but instead must keep self-optimising. 'Never too sick to work, never too sad, never too besieged by familial obligations, never heartsick, never traumatised by the images that surround them, never existentially fearful for the future of the planet, but endlessly resilient, endlessly striving, endlessly motivated by more money because somehow, no matter how much you have of it, you never feel secure enough,' Petersen writes. Even in trying and failing to fulfil this role as an ideal worker, 'you only solidify it as an ideal'.

I want to deconstruct myself as any kind of worker, regardless of whether I am eventually made into a mother or a woman without children. I am apprehensive now about the relentless, goal-oriented, outcome-obsessed, self-interested texture of paid employment as most of us know it folding into any part of my future. Sorry to the women who dreamed of taking their aprons off to go to university so I could imagine staying in my dressing gown a little longer each day, pursuing mediocrity in each part of my life.

In love, we find who we are, in devotion we express it. Love can mean recognising all mothers as working mothers. Love can mean solidarity, organising for security and conditions or valuing care work. Love can mean regarding a human as more than a speck of capital whose interests will rarely align with anyone who seeks to exploit them as such. Love does not begin as labour and it exists beyond it.

5

Emotional labour

I was one of the 237,000 people who laughed and hit 'like' on this tweet by @kylieGjansen in 2020: 'happy mother's day to every straight guy's first 3-4 girlfriends.'

It feels like an uncool time to consider irreversibly and indefinitely tethering yourself to a straight man by creating a child together. If you spend enough time online, writes academic Yuhe Faye Wong, you get the sense that heterosexuality is on the way out. 'Among a particular set (woke social justice warriors), it is a truth universally acknowledged that heterosexuality is a prison, a form of Stockholm syndrome for women cursed to date men,' Wong writes. The internet is rife with what Indiana Seresin calls heteropessimism – 'performative disaffiliations with heterosexuality, usually expressed in the form of regret, embarrassment, or hopelessness about straight experience'.

No one is in good faith claiming it is inconvenient to be aligned with the most normalised sexual orientation, particularly when it comes to family-making, or oppressive to pass as straight courtesy of your relationship, just that heterosexuality as an institution is looking a bit worse for wear.

Unlike those spouting vile homophobia and transphobia online, people who have turned the question 'are straight people okay?' into a catchphrase, have good reason to be concerned. A news story about a woman whose husband told her to 'shush' while she was in labour. Are straight people okay? A gender reveal party firework that sparked a wildfire, forcing hundreds of people to flee their homes. Are straight people okay? A *New York Times* article titled 'How I Trained My Husband To Be A Dad'. Are straight people okay? A T-shirt that says *My favourite Disney villain is my wife*. Are straight people okay? An entire interior design article explaining to women which items in their home might be off-putting to men (cactuses are 'unwelcoming' while art or vases featuring individual women might wrongly imply you're happier single). Are straight people okay?

Straight men bear the brunt of the bewilderment. There are endless posts ridiculing behaviours deemed to belong to them. They have loud cars and loud sneezes, they call each other by their last names, they wear long board shorts, they love to spit on the ground, they walk up the stairs two at a time, they lie about being 6 foot, their skincare regime is just soap, they believe they're not sexist because their girlfriend is a woman, they believe they're not sexist because their mother is a woman, they don't clean their fingernails, they're in leadership positions but can't cook a microwave meal, they do the bare minimum and receive unending praise from their partners and society at large.

In between the justifiable mockery of abusive men, incels and trolls, there are infinite jokes in which straight men play teenage boys and the women dating them are patient mothers.

They fit roughly into two cartoonish archetypes. The man who is hopelessly emotionally inexpressive, intent on adhering to bizarre codes of masculinity, clueless, lazy, out of touch with himself and unable to connect with women – @blairsocci tweeted during the pandemic, 'My heart goes out to men whom without sports are feeling their feelings for the first time instead of yelling at the screen welcome bitch here's a white wine'. He's the unromantic boyfriend, the doltish sitcom patriarch for whom patience is waning, the jock we now demand vulnerability from. The other broad category is a man who is more emotionally literate or at least has the vocabulary to appear so but expresses too much, too soon and he is ridiculed in the same way women often are – for being needy, clingy, oversharing, sensitive, easily offended, at best delicate, at worst manipulative but importantly still selfish and unable to treat women well – *Reductress*: 'Clever! Man Co-Opting Social Justice Language to Emotionally Abuse You'. These men and their variants blend into the same virtual portrait of a man who has unreasonable needs and an underripe ability to respect boundaries, to care and to communicate. A friend discovers single women using donor sperm are the fastest growing segment of the assisted reproduction market and tweets: 'I'm assuming this is because it is easier to raise one baby rather than two.'

You can almost hear the chorus of snickering and knowing groans across keyboards, a virtual but genuine solidarity in the shared weariness and wariness of dating men. If this was a story about bad men or male entitlement it would fit neatly into 240 characters.

I understand that parental love should be unconditional and that the care of a child can be unrelenting and unreciprocated and go unrecognised. You are there to catch your child's emotions when they come all at once and when they are withheld and hard to read. I expect a child needs you to communicate patiently and intuit their needs attentively. Your value is in what you do, not who you are because your primary function for them is to keep them safe and supported so they can grow in every way. What I want to understand is how this dynamic has been woven into our romantic relationships and why. I want to know why so many women feel obliged to be the main provider of emotional security for their partners. In patriarchal culture, love becomes a resource, something men should 'receive without expending effort', writes author bell hooks. 'More often than not they do not want to do the work that love demands.' Despite the reductive tweets, most women I know are not at risk of procreating with a grunting boofhead or manipulative man-child. They are instead depleted by the most traditional and tiring features in their otherwise progressive relationships and worry how bearable these patterns would be in parenthood.

Within many heterosexual relationships, this imbalance creates a simmering resentment. For better or worse, millennial women can feel responsible for our own well-being and, since we've been encouraged to treat the self as an enterprise, our own personal growth. For many, our 20s were a process of maturing, introspecting, sharing our thoughts and feelings with each other, and sometimes a professional, and moving in and out of relationships with people who were yet to learn to do the same. We found the words, not just in snide tweets but in tired group chats, to describe the aftermath of what hooks says is the first act of violence that patriarchy demands of men: 'That they engage in acts of psychic self-mutilation, that they kill off the emotional parts of themselves.' We begrudged the ministrations that fell to the person in a relationship who was not encouraged to amputate but rather overwork and strengthen the emotional part of herself until it was muscular enough to carry another person. The one who had spent her adult life confronting, understanding and improving the ability to communicate her own feelings and patterns of behaviour, reckoning with past trauma and practising leaning on others for support. The partner who was already more likely to do the majority of the household labour became the partner more likely to take on the bulk of care and communication. The one who then not only became the human list, calendar, alarm, diary, schedule, reminder, booking system, archive and point of contact for their partner (and any potential offspring) but also the person who must start and finish hard conversations.

'Managing your partner's emotions – anticipating needs, preempting displeasure, and keeping the peace – is something women are taught to accept as their duty from an early age,' writes Gemma Hartley. Many of my friends and I, most of whom are childless, have taken on unpaid organising or caretaking and been made to feel this comes more 'naturally' to us, until the assumption self-fulfils. A housemate once glanced up from playing *FIFA* to encourage me to finally 'write the book about mothering'. He had not done a weekly chore in three months but I smiled and thanked him for the encouragement as I walked up the stairs I had mopped earlier that day. I could fill pages about just physical unpaid domestic labour – of which women do nearly three times as much as men – but it is often the invisible, ill-defined emotional labour I want to understand. By the time we're nearing our 30s, my friends and I have been in relationships, even fleeting ones, with men in which the division of care and communication was so asymmetrical that for most of our 20s we arrived at each other's houses lopsided, ready to vent until our spines were straight again. We've all been among the straight guy's first three to four girlfriends.

A friend tells me her Italian family uses the phrase *mente fresca*, meaning a fresh mind, a clear-headedness you can default to. '*Mente fresca, mente fresca,*' she repeats it like a directive. Since becoming a mother she finds herself thinking about all of the men in her life who 'get to be *mente fresca*' about most things. 'They are only burdened by the things they allow themselves to be burdened by.' She fantasises about what would happen if she stopped taking mental responsibility for the laundry, the food, the sleep schedules, the appointments. 'But it can't be more than a thought experiment because I have a baby that depends on me to keep him alive.'

Sociologist Arlie Russell Hochschild, who coined the term 'emotional labour' in the 1980s to describe the managing of one's own emotions expected of workers in certain professions, has said while the term can apply to relationships, it is being wrongly used for a range of household tasks or romantic functions. Modern usage of the term has drifted far from any recognition of class relations but I think it was pinched because there weren't yet the words for what we now describe this way. I consider how we might keep these emotional tasks intact, attached to their genuinely loving origins while tearing them from their default association to women in relationships with men. It can be hard under capitalism to evaluate emotional labour without becoming a resentful ledger-keeper who sees love and care as commodities to be transacted. But there's an undeniable atmosphere in which, for many women in relationships with men, the thought of starting a family feels daunting because they are already depleted by the relationship, however loving. Not sometimes drained in the way networks of reciprocal love and care might ideally ebb and flow but constantly at a loss. Motherhood does not promise to balance the sheet.

When I first turned up at a psychologist as a teenager, I was there to figure out how to survive the mental illness and addiction that was destabilising my home. This doctor had proven himself a wizard, magicking away my night terrors with a kind of hypnosis. He helped me learn a language with which I could articulate feelings to myself in times of paralysing fear and fathomless depression. I trusted him completely. Although I knew by that age I no longer believed in God, I didn't mind that he was a Catholic; in fact, I secretly hoped, as if by osmosis, I might absorb something holy by being near him. I welcomed his belief in the sanctity of life, a bracingly simple and helpfully abrupt response to my suicidal ideation. 'How lucky are we to be in this body, on this earth? Life is far too precious to give away in a moment,' he said dismissively. But there was one appointment, the only one I remember clearly, in which his religiosity cemented my ideas about how I believed men and women should give and receive care. I have been trying to unlearn it ever since.

I knew even as a teenager that the feelings I described in this appointment were obvious and unoriginal. I told him I felt like I could never shine brightly enough or else make myself small and needless enough to be worthy of the same love and attention I felt my brothers had earned

172

through their personal struggles. I described for the first time a cloak of unwanted anonymity within my family that only slipped off when I felt worthlessness. In other words, I only felt visible when I felt like I'd failed. I followed this disclosure up with a guilty rant about how I knew this wasn't actually important and that my mother, our primary carer, had enough on her plate with four kids and I was lucky not to need much consideration. I asked him how I might show my parents how clever and strong I was without inconveniencing them.

The psychologist did not dwell on either of my requests and instead he spoke for the rest of the session about the Virgin Mary. He spoke of her as Our Lady of Sorrows, or the Sorrowful Mother, depicted in Catholic imagery with seven daggers piercing her heart. Each sword, he explained to me, represented each of the sorrows she felt about her son, Jesus. 'That is how mothers love their sons,' he said. He seemed touched by the archetypal mother's pain, which he said was present on her face in every depiction of this Catholic devotion. Jacqueline Rose describes the image of the tortured mother, particularly the Virgin Mary grieving her dead son, as a stable of maternal imagery. 'With the suffering of the whole world etched on her face, she carries and assuages the burden of human misery on behalf of everyone,' Rose writes. The psychologist made explicit that the love a mother has for her son is unavoidably consuming and inherently painful – see the blood seeping from her wounded heart, see her grief-stricken gaze – and in this he made implicit what I'd already been socialised to believe for years: that a daughter should be forever self-reliant, a grown-up while growing up, a martyr-in-waiting, a rock in a river, and always unarmed – after all, there's nowhere on Mary's heart left to wound. My housemate gets a package from her mother in her home country. The note reads: *Thank you for taking such good care of yourself for me.*

The psychologist encouraged me to find a church where I might find this image in a stained glass window or a sculpture and to kneel before it and meditate on the fact that I can't change that I'm a daughter but that that was okay.

Leslie Jamison captures the danger in assuming that female pain is inevitable. 'We risk transforming their suffering from an aspect of the female experience into an element of the female constitution – perhaps its finest, frailest consummation,' she writes. I was uniquely primed to believe, as she describes, that suffering, particularly in service of men you love, is the 'unending glue and prerequisite of female consciousness'.

An ex-boyfriend told me that when he was about to get his tattoos, his mother, distraught about the idea, offered her own body up instead to be inked, wanting his skin to remain as unblemished as it was when she'd created him. Throughout our relationship, I told his mother repeatedly that I didn't want children but she asked again and again and again in different ways when I might. 'Do you love spending time with your gorgeous niece and nephew?' she asked pointedly.

'Yes, so much, and I enjoy handing them back,' I responded, smiling. I was a uterus; an invisible site of unfertilised potential. She drove us to the airport after we visited. Bags out, boot closed, time for goodbyes.

She hugged me too tight and whispered, 'Take *care* of him,' slipping an invisible baton into my hand for the next leg of the relay. I didn't know it yet but I would delight in this race then, somehow, resent it. I would fail miserably, eventually returning him back into her superior care with a broken heart. In every relationship with a man I learned that I am not infinite as I'd learned mothers must be. I discovered that my reluctance to cause men discomfort, to trust that they will survive my boundaries, to have my own needs and then express them clearly does not make for honest or equal relationships. Only a child thrives on care that is given out of obligation, and I want to believe that most men are not boys. But they once were.

Dr Judy Y Chu's research shows that conditioning men to be invulnerable starts very early. Her two-year study followed boys from pre-kindergarten through to first grade and found many tenets of masculinity – emotional stoicism, aggression, inexpressiveness or social ineptitude – aren't innate but a learned performance. These boys desired close relationships and were able to express their emotions as well as little girls but by age five or six, they had learned to publicly discard these skills and reject or hide friendships with girls. 'Both boys and girls are born with a capacity for and a fundamental desire for relationships – to be close and to be connected and if anything they find that boy babies need more help regulating themselves,' Chu told *The Atlantic*. 'When they are upset they need their primary caregiver to help them regulate and come back to a feeling of contentment.' She points out that while infant studies show all kids seek connection to others, later studies show adolescent boys reporting fewer close relationships and lower levels of intimacy. 'They start out wanting and thriving in relationships, and then they are moved away from those protective relationships, and there's a cost.'

Psychologist and former president of the Society for the Psychological Study of Men and Masculinities Dr Andrew Smiler says that because boys in Western English-speaking cultures are not taught to express their feelings, they are implicitly encouraged not to pay attention to them. 'Why pay attention to something you are not going to address?' he asks. Smiler writes that the person in a partnership who is more knowledgeable about feelings and relationships will become 'the relationship expert' who 'invests more time and energy in strengthening the relationship and smoothing out its rough spots'. The ideal of men as problem-solvers encourages them to do instead of to be or to feel. 'This is epitomised in our tendency to ask men, "what are you going to do about it?" instead of "how do you feel about it?"' I learned early on in journalism that you're more likely to get an interviewee who is a man to tell you how he feels about something by asking him what he thinks about it.

The Most Important Job in the World

My understanding of masculinity as a hard rock that has only recently softened enough to take new forms is ahistorical, according to Smiler. Unlike in the 1800s, when he says men were permitted to display passion and affection in their friendships with other men, our late 20th century version of masculinity, is more 'explicitly toxic'. He argues this masculinity specifically supports men's violence, aggression and risk-taking and directs men to minimise certain aspects of human-functioning, such as emotional expression and connections with others. 'Many of these men claim that it is better to be angry or aggressive than to express other feelings,' he writes.

I want to understand the rules. Robert Brannon and Deborah David's 'man box' – a definition of the evolved industrial model of masculinity that we have all encountered – consists of four principles. The first is 'no sissy stuff', or avoid engaging in behaviours or displaying traits that are associated with femininity like displaying emotions or relying on others. The second is 'be a big wheel' – use your ambition and competitiveness to strive for status and success. The third, 'be a sturdy oak', instructs you to function independently from others and to speak through actions, not through feelings. The fourth is what they refer to as 'damn the torpedoes, full speed ahead', which is the directive that men be decisive, take risks and display aggression, adventurousness and fearlessness. It was strange to read these rules and know immediately how they applied to the men in my life while simultaneously seeing how they were also the basis of a kind of aggressive corporatised feminism, in which women are encouraged to adopt the most power-hungry and inhuman aspects of masculinity in order to access what men have. I can see how these traits, none of which are exclusively or consistently bad, are impossible to follow all the time as a member of a social species with emotional needs.

Associate Professor Michael Flood, who researches men, masculinities and violence prevention at Queensland University of Technology, used the man box in his research. He found that belief in stereotypical masculine norms among men aged 18 to 30 is around an astounding 20 times more important than demographic variables like education, occupation and ethnicity in predicting the use of physical violence, sexual harassment and online bullying. Endorsement of these masculine norms was 11 times more influential than other factors in predicting binge drinking and ten times more influential in predicting negative mood. Suicidal thoughts were associated most strongly with men's conformity to 'hypersexuality' and 'self-sufficiency' including agreement with the statement: 'Men should figure out their personal problems on their own without asking others for help.'

'One of the key lessons that is part of traditional masculine socialisation is to repress emotions, particularly emotions that indicate vulnerability or weakness. So anger is legitimate and capable of being expressed but more vulnerable emotions of fear or distress or hurt are punished and associated with femininity and one of the key lessons that boys and men still learn is that "above all we should not be women",' Flood tells me. 'That then plays itself out in men's lack of emotional reflectiveness, lack of emotional skill and in unequal divisions of emotional work.'

Flood is quick to identify that women experience 'frustration, dissatisfaction, emotional exhaustion, burnout' from these imbalances. I expect us to spend some time talking about the way these rules might disadvantage men in relationships with women, as his work so clearly shows these masculine norms don't benefit the men who abide by them. Instead he only points out that men themselves might lose out if their partners have less relationship and sexual satisfaction and if their partners eventually leave them. 'Of course, there are advantages and privileges for the person who is doing less in the same way that if they are doing less childcare and less housework,' he tells me. 'The benefits of time and space and also the benefits of attention to your emotional needs and having your emotional needs looked after . . . If you're not spending time thinking about how the other partner is going and what they are facing and how you can support them, then you have more time for your own leisure and paid work and your own emotional needs.' Even as an academic who has spent years studying and thinking about masculinity, Flood says he is still discovering the ways in which his gender impacts the emotional health of his own relationship. 'I have poorer emotional literacy than her,' he admits. 'I am poorer at recognising my own emotions and expressing what is going on for me . . . In the past, I've often said I feel a bit flat and I've been pushed by her to come up with more adjectives, to come up with a richer and more diverse language than "flat". I've realised that "flat" can be I'm angry or frustrated or despondent or sad or embarrassed or guilty or lonely. There are all kinds of emotions that flat can conceal.'

Movember director and clinical psychologist Dr Zac Seidler, who works mostly with men, says often patients come in and say they just broadly feel 'shit'. He gets out a big wheel with different colours and adjectives on it to figure out what kind of 'shit' they might be feeling.

I'm stunned by the simplicity of this. I want to ask if the men find this patronising but I know it is the wrong question. 'It sounds like they're learning a new language?' I offer instead.

'It is exactly that,' he says. 'They have the adjectives they would just never use them to describe their emotional experience but I always say, "I don't want you to talk in any way that is not comfortable for you" and "I'm not going to get you to put words to things that don't make sense. I want you to describe it in a way that is useful to you."' Seidler works with his clients to break down physical sensations like sweaty hands or a racing heart to help determine feelings like 'anxious'. 'I'll pick up that there is clear discomfort in them saying, like, "nervous" or "blue" or whatever it may be and so I'll ask, "Why does that feel so uncomfortable?" and they'll talk about stigma or they'll say I feel weak in saying that or guilty because people are worse off,' he says. 'It's called emotion coaching, and we do it with children and you do an adult version I guess with guys who are really struggling.'

I call a friend who has a one-year-old. She struggles to know what to do with her partner's emotions, which he can rarely name. Their communication always reaches 'a natural dead-end' beyond which he can't be reflective or specific about his emotions, but now they have a child there is even less time to find a way back to each other. 'Now it is laid bare every day,' she says.

I think about emotions that aren't verbally expressed as what they are, how sadness, worry and fear can look like anger, irritability, frustration, obsession, possessiveness, inertia. I think about how a child does not need to articulate their precise emotion for parents to identify there is a need. I think about what I would do if I was struggling to name an emotion and realise I do this regularly. I take time to diagnose anger. I feel like it is not an emotion that I am allowed to feel, much less express. It can take me some time to know it is there and I then usually take it to the only place it can be expressed without censorship or judgement – a group chat of women. I read through the flashes of anger in our messages. Brief flares that disappear between the videos of birds and cats and links to long-form articles we want to read, skanky tops we want to buy and TikToks we want to laugh at. A voice memo that begins, 'sorry but . . .' Are we also guilty of cleaving off parts of ourselves and sharing them in privacy away from our partners? Does it matter?

There's a reason when men have a gender preference when choosing a therapist, it is a woman, Seidler says. 'If you only go to your mum to talk about your emotions, then you end up getting mothered by your partner and that is where it starts,' he says. 'You need to see your dad and grandpa talk and express emotions early on because this stuff gets locked in so quickly.'

I ask Seidler about relationships where a man's girl-friend might be the only person he is vulnerable with. 'I guess if she's got a therapist and a huge circle of friends she can talk to without shame it gives his vulnerability this kind of weight?' I ask.

'Exactly! You've got everyone to lean on and you have everyone to have those connections with,' he says. But the heaviness of this responsibility doesn't make many women I know feel special; in fact, there is a sense of anonymity in relationships with men who need a lot of emotional care-taking. The speed and intensity at which he wants to be soothed or comforted doesn't track a genuine intimacy in which each person is learning about the other.

My friend Hayley has often observed, 'This guy doesn't actually know me so it isn't me he thinks he's falling in love with, he just likes how I make him *feel*.' This sense that your value is in your output not in your personhood feeds the comparison to mothering – a child needs the care of his parents but is rarely interested in their inner life. Hayley describes feeling like a kind of hybrid mother-therapist, 'even in one-night stands' somehow.

'I'm helping them to process their emotions, work out why they're feeling a certain way or why they reacted a certain way, show them what they're suppressing or resenting me or other people for, teach them how to respond better in a situation of conflict with a workmate or something and often show them how they are unfairly judging their ex-girlfriend's side of the story,' she says. 'They'll say things like, "you make me a better person", "you understand me", "you make me comfortable", "you make me realise things I've never realised before", "you've taught me so much", "you're the only person I can or have ever spoken to about these things".'

The Australian Housewives' Manual (1883) said: '[Your husband] sleeps as securely as a child, simply because you have nourished him, soothed him, and driven away every trace of care and discomfort.' Even though research shows men are just as likely as women to want emotional intimacy in their friendships, 25 per cent of men aged 30 to 64 had no one outside of their immediate family they felt they could rely on. Heterosexual white men have the fewest friends of anyone in America, and this isolation worsens in early parenthood – an increasing number of fathers lose contact with close friends in the first year of welcoming a child, which worsens stress levels. Who meets your social and emotional needs when your family unit contracts around a child?

The responsibility to be the sole witness to your partner's emotion, once glorified as a gift – 'it is only by quiet devotion that you will win his confidence and become the partaker of his innermost thoughts . . . his reliance on you will know no bounds' the housewives' manual claims – has become characterised as a burden, in many ways because it is presumed to not weigh anything at all.

'[The effort of emotional work] has commonly been overlooked because they have tended to be characterised as reflections of interpersonal intimacy or love,' sociology professor Rebecca Erickson writes in the conclusion of her research on the topic. 'Caregiving, in whatever form, does not just emanate from within, but must be managed, focused, and directed so as to have the intended effect on the care recipient.' Hayley's describing short-term dalliances with often subjectively insignificant others but in the moment she feels what any human being would: a responsibility to handle someone's feelings with tender attention. For years I've watched this play out in her encounters with guy after guy, and even though I know she doesn't want a boyfriend, as an outsider it seems as though in each situation the best parts of a fling – heat, spontaneity, independence, freedom from expectations and explanations – are eventually eclipsed by the one-way responsibility for someone else's emotional stability. As a *Reductress* headline smirked: '"I'm Not Looking For Anything Serious," Says Man Who Will Rely on You for All His Emotional Support'.

'There are also the small things, like reminding them to eat or get a good night's sleep or calming them down when they're angry or stressed and there is the constant, constant,

constant listening to them rant about themselves or people who have wronged them,' Hayley says. 'It isn't a conversation, just a one-way monologue about themselves . . . it's not reciprocated but I know they can't actually help me in the way I help them.'

Hayley is one of the few friends I know who rejected the idea that a partner must be a neat mosaic of what we seek in all our human relationships. Instead she found emotional intimacy in her friends, romance in prose, intellectual stimulation in her study, financial stability in her work and in doing so managed to make it through her 20s without much heartbreak or regret. She has never been bothered by the fact that these people weren't right to build a life with but now at 30, she is considering what a future with one person might look like and whether that involves children. The only type of man she has been with all expect her to perform a role she would never sign up for long-term.

Erickson's study unsurprisingly found that men who held a more traditional gender ideology were more likely to perform less emotion work and their wives were more likely to perform more childcare. I don't often try things I'm unpractised at either. Hayley embodies many 'masculine' ideals, including stoicism and competitiveness, and she isn't someone I would describe as people-pleasing. Erikson's study found applying more feminine-expressive traits to oneself was associated with the performance of more emotion work among women but even women who saw themselves in masculine terms were more likely to perform emotion work. In other words, no woman seemed immune to the far-reaching impacts of gender norms. Hayley is remarkably independent and since we were kids, I've watched her take complete responsibility for herself. She has read countless philosophy and psychology books, she has meditated and practised yoga, she has thought deeply about how her family structure has shaped who she is, she has journalled, and she has contemplated how her own tendencies and behaviours will impact her needs in all of her relationships. Whenever I arc up about how immaturely these men are behaving, Hayley will laugh and shake her head and say, in the voice of a mother, something like, 'What can you do? They don't know any better.' She sometimes feels like she has left these men better than she found them for the next woman. At the tail-end of every one of these encounters – at the outset of which the man, pre-empting that fabled feminine cling-iness, has insisted there will be 'no strings attached' – I find myself observing again that she is doing the work of the girlfriend without any of the perks. There is none of the two-way care one might expect in a stable monogamous relationship and instead a denial that anything exhausting is underway – how could it be after all? This isn't exclusive, you're not my girlfriend, you're not my wife. Hayley and I often talk about how avoidable this would be if the guy had been previously emotionally intimate with someone other than their mothers, or sometimes ex-girlfriends. If he had been encouraged to introspect before he was approach-ing, or in some cases surpassing, 30, he wouldn't be having these epiphanies with a near stranger at 2 am in his bed, on which hours before she had put the sheets – 'I honestly don't think he knew how.'

Seidler says there is no evidence boys are somehow innately unable to experience and express a full range of emotions. 'You slowly watch this restriction and closing in boys' emotional experience to the point where they start to fully cut off a part of themselves, which is so terribly sad,' he says. 'If you don't have that ability and don't practise, you lose capacity and confidence . . . it is not condoned and the people around them are not asking for it and don't know how to respond to it.' Romantic relationships 'open up a man's emotional spectrum', Seidler says. 'Which is shit scary . . . They feel things they haven't felt before and they can't name them and their partner is pushing them for descriptions of love which have been literally drilled out of them over time.' Seidler describes a subclinical phenomenon called alexithymia, derived from Greek meaning having no words for emotions. *A* (lack) – *lexis* (word) – *thymos* (emotions). 'Lots of the research suggests there is a thing called male normative alexithymia, as in it is the norm for guys to not be able to do this,' he says. 'What I tell lots of our male clients is that that restriction means they lose the potential to express and describe grief and sadness but they also lose joy and they lose lightness and they lose fun.'

He remembers a male patient who came in and was talking about his relationship problems and Seidler asked him what ran through his head during the conflict. The man responded, '"What do you mean?" I said, "What do you think to yourself? What comes to mind? What do you reflect on? Do you chastise yourself? Do you get angry with yourself, do you reflect in any way?" And he goes, "I don't understand" and it became very clear very quickly that he does not have an internal voice . . . I could not comprehend how he never reflected on things.' Seidler said although his relationship was in disrepair, the man was 'mentally healthy'. 'He just hadn't honed that skill and so I talked him through that and he started to build it up over time.'

While women are more likely to suffer from severe stress and anxiety, one in seven Australian men experiences depression or anxiety or both in any year, and Australian men are three times more likely to die by suicide than women, yet evidence indicates men are far less likely to seek help for mental health conditions. Despite this, Seidler says not enough clinicians are doing the hard yards early on in appointments to orient their male patients to a foreign system. He makes clear the practical outcomes of treatment and uses language that is about taking action and problem solving. 'I empower him to change and understand his responsibility here and that's a way of leveraging masculinity by explaining that he is in control and he is the expert,' he says. 'I say it's going to be tough but that is what bravery is and that is what courage is.' He uses the metaphor of a personal trainer – you might see him for an hour a week, but if you don't work out in between, you won't get results. Seidler wants there to be more realistic depictions in media and art of men in therapy so men come in willingly. 'It is always like Woody Allen lying on a couch being neurotic and talking about his mother,' he says, laughing. 'I see so many men that have been forced in by their partners and mothers and they don't want to be there and I need to give them a reason to connect, a reason to gain skills that is not doing it for someone else.'

Men are far less likely to seek professional help and are far less likely to lean on their friends for emotional support, so his partner might be trying to provide all the support a community should.

As I write this in 2020, there is a trend on Twitter of tweets about things men would rather do than see a mental health professional – 'get a whole new girlfriend' instead of going to therapy, 'unnecessarily reverse into a parking space' instead of going to therapy, 'watch hours of James Gandolfini going to therapy on *The Sopranos*' instead of going to therapy, 'start a new workout routine' instead of going to therapy and 'literally run for president' instead of going to therapy. 'If there's one thing a girl with a bad boyfriend has, it's the moral upper hand in the religion of mental health,' writes Kristin Dombek. This piousness can be useful when your friend has left a relationship with a man who has refused to take responsibility for himself – she can bubble with indignation like it is hot oil, frying any lingering crumbs of care or concern to a crisp. She can move on. But the upper hands of women with ostensibly *good* boyfriends, with whom they'd like to remain and maybe even procreate, are strained from overuse. A 2020 study of hundreds of same-sex and different-sex marriages found that providing 'emotion work' in relationships reduces the psychological wellbeing of the person providing it, especially when the spouse and recipient of the care has elevated depressive symptoms and when one's spouse is a man.

'There has to be something more than therapy,' a friend says to me, rebuking the flood of online pleas from women for men to sort out their mental health instead of bringing it into the relationship. We talk about this imperative to pay for what we don't want to ask of others and what it might mean for our sense of community and accountability. I don't want someone else to have to outsource and privatise their mental health, as I've watched so many women do. I'd rather people of all genders grow up feeling comfortable enough to talk to their friends, partners and a professional, if needed. Seidler says men are ready to talk about their feelings but people aren't willing to listen. 'We did this study at Movember where over 80 per cent of guys are comfortable and wanting to open up about their emotions to someone in their life, 41 per cent who had done so to a friend, family member or doctor and had a really shit time and were not going to do it again,' he says. 'We end up with this group of men who go, "Alright, I was willing to, I gave it a go and they just didn't know what to do with it."'

Shame researcher Brené Brown says shame itself is gendered – women's shame comes from not meeting multiple conflicting and unrealistic expectations, while men's shame comes from showing weakness. While the women I know want their partners to feel safe and supported when expressing difficult emotions, Brown believes we're failing at it. 'The truth is that most women can't stomach it,' she writes. 'In those moments when real vulnerability happens in men, most of us recoil with fear, and that fear manifests as everything from disappointment to disgust.'

This notion makes me bristle with a kind of defensiveness because I have tried and failed to recall feeling disgust or disappointment when a man has shown emotion and, with admittedly smug relief, I find that I can't relate to the feeling at all. This isn't to say I haven't internalised other unrealistic expectations of men or that I haven't been judgemental when a man has resorted to *other* coping mechanisms to deal with his emotions – minimisation, substances, aggression, violence, denial or avoidance. Just as I believe many men have accepted the narrative that women must be caring and are disappointed when their nurturers have needs, I know many women are following a script that casts men as unflinchingly stoic and can feel unequipped in the face of their emotionality. When I think about the instances when my friends feel a kind of disappointment or disgust with their partners, it hasn't been a momentary recoiling from disclosures of emotion, which they understand as flashes of bravery. It has been a diffusion of their desire as it trickles down the very asymmetrical slope I am trying to understand.

I recall a series of conversations I've had with many friends in relationships with men over the years about how assuming a caretaker role impacts the way you perceive your partner. It wasn't until our mid-20s when we discovered and subsequently developed a parasocial relationship with Belgian psychotherapist Esther Perel that we found the language for it. Her work attempts to explain how the demands of modern monogamy – 'we expect one person to give us what once an entire village used to provide, and we live twice as long' – is a series of tensions between security and space, surrender and autonomy, the domestic and the erotic. 'Love likes to shrink the distance that exists between me and you, while desire is energised by it,' she writes, or as she often puts it 'fire needs air'. Perel believes balancing these contradictions is the central challenge of modern relationships at a point in history when individuals more often enter into marriage as a romantic rather than an economic partnership. 'Caretaking is the most powerful anti-aphrodisiac for women,' Perel says. 'If I am in caretaking mode, I am in mothering mode, not lovemaking mode. I am in taking-care-of-others mode.' Cue a series of 'omg this' texts. This is part of the reason women can need more foreplay or time to transition into a state of mind compatible with sex. Perel says it takes a moment to reorient one's attention from meeting other people's needs to focusing on your own, and feeling selfish enough to have them met. This is a time-sensitive example, but it is helpful to speak of 'modes' because the problem for many women is the structure of their relationship forces them into caretaker mode close to full-time, often before they even have kids. As Perel puts it, 'It's hard to experience desire when you're weighted down by concern.' The unabating *if I don't do it, it won't get done because he won't think to or doesn't know how* mantra means women can't frequently move in and out of care-taking mode as many husbands and fathers can. In other words, she's not turned off by soothing her boyfriend, she's turned off by repeatedly soothing a man who, like a child, expects and needs her as he can't or won't ever find comfort elsewhere. This isn't necessarily a problem of how much or what types of care someone is taking on in a heterosexual relationship – there are plenty of women who want to take on these types of tasks – it is about whether that care was deliberately divided by two adults or unthinkingly and silently assigned based on gender expectations.

Seidler has no time for the phrase 'toxic masculinity', a 'media-invented term' that he says offers us nothing. There are parts of traditional or hegemonic masculinity that can be beneficial and protective, he argues. 'Stoicism and silence and getting the fuck on with it sometimes is going to be really useful for you in an evolutionary perspective when there is a crisis happening as long as when you come out of the fire you can reflect on it and cry and talk to your wife about it and do the work,' he says. 'We need to have masculinities, plural, and embrace that they are contradictory and they coalesce and change over time between and within men. We need to be able to open up to masculinities moment to moment.' He describes one of his patients, a towering, tattooed builder. 'If I based my treatment plan on how he looked and spoke in the first 15 minutes, I'd have locked into the idea that he was a traditional man. In fact, over time, he was the most emotionally in-tune man I'd ever met and it changed between sessions, he would go back to being rough as shit and then he would go into being lovely and soft and crying.'

We are in the midst of a gender reckoning, says Seidler, and men are stuck, trying to straddle between new and old expectations of masculinity. 'It is like, be vulnerable, be emotional, describe everything that is going on for you, be a better father, be soft, be caring, and then as well as that do all of the traditional things, don't lose them because we don't know how to get rid of patriarchy and masculinity,' he says. 'They feel like they're constantly failing at both.'

I think of my friend ranting, 'I just want [my boyfriend] to communicate with me more often and not in these big bursts when he's really at a low or when he's drunk.'

'*Is that unreasonable?*' I find myself wondering. There aren't enough public examples of men who can comfortably move between these masculinities, Seidler says, which is why young men are buying up *12 Rules For Life: An Antidote To Chaos* by self-help guru Jordan Peterson, who believes 'the masculine spirit is under assault' by social progress and that good women should be 'conscientious and agreeable'. 'Peterson is selling a male doctrine for living and it plays into masculinity because it goes, "here are the rules, just follow them you'll be sweet",' Seidler says. Nor is it hard to see why comedian Joe Rogan, whose podcasts have almost 200 million monthly downloads, is capturing this demographic. As writer Devin Gordon, who spent six weeks immersed in the world of Rogan put it, these men are aware of their privilege but are 'sick of being reminded of it' and feel 'thwarted and besieged and sentenced to an endless apology tour'. Seidler says Rogan plays on the fact that his audience feel under siege, and that while they have the patriarchy behind them, they don't *feel* supported. '[A Rogan listener] doesn't feel powerful; he feels disenfranchised,' Seidler says.

'Right,' I respond. 'So it is kind of a situation where equality can feel like oppression if you're the person who stands to lose power?'

'Men are starting to go, "Wait a minute, we are not being benefited by the patriarchy", and sadly it has taken and is going to continue to take women to push for change,' Seidler says. 'The way out of this gender reckoning is for men to realise amongst each other that they need to do some of this work and women will prop them up, naturally, because they want to see it happen.'

I make another note at the end of the interview: *prop them up naturally*. I slowly circle the word *naturally*.

A 2019 study examining the association of marital strain with psychological distress in gay, lesbian and heterosexual marriages found that women in different-sex marriages reported the highest levels of psychological distress while men in same-sex marriages reported the lowest. Those outside of heterosexuality were asking whether straight people are okay long before the memes. 'Not only for our own sake – because we fear homophobic violence or erasure of queer subculture – but also because straight culture's impact on straight women often elicits our confusion and distress,' Jane Ward writes. This isn't to say living under the cultural weight of heteronormativity isn't hard when you don't fit within it, Ward writes, nor is it to say queer people don't hurt each other. 'But the key difference between straight culture and queer culture in this regard is that the latter does not attribute these destructive behaviours to a romantic story about a natural and inescapable gender binary.'

What does parenthood look like beyond that fairytale? 'When it comes to parenting, the fact that same-sex parents can't slide into default gender patterns creates some striking differences,' Stephanie Coontz, author of *Marriage: A History*, writes, noting that surveys consistently find that men married to women spend the least amount of total time and the lowest proportion of their nonwork time engaged with their kids. A survey of hundreds of dual-earner couples found same-sex couples tended to share more duties and assign various chores based on personal preference while straight couples slipped into traditional gender roles, with women, lower earners, and those with fewer work hours taking primary responsibility for stereotypical female chores like laundry. It found same-sex couples were twice as likely to share child-care duties. This doesn't mean same-sex couples don't assign specialised roles based on relative (to their partner) socioeconomic factors; in fact, research shows they do so more often after they become parents. 'Though the couples are still more equitable, one partner often has higher earnings, and one a greater share of household chores and child care,' Claire Cain Miller writes. 'It shows these roles are not just about gender.' Research finds even when they don't divide labour equitably, gay and lesbian couples are more likely to find their division fair. A 12-year comparison of how couples initiate and handle disagreements found that while overall relationship satisfaction and quality was roughly the same across all groups, when it came to conflict, gay and lesbian couples used fewer 'controlling, hostile emotional tactics' and displayed 'less belligerence, domineering and fear' with each other than straight couples did. The Gottman Institute study found they used more affection and humour to resolve conflict and were better at soothing one another.

In a depressing op-ed for the *New York Times*, in which she encourages mothers to keep a 'martyr log' of situations when they've gone to unreasonable lengths to make life easy for their family, perinatal psychiatrist Dr Pooja Lakshmin says she sees women who are struggling to meet the demands of their roles at work and home. She calls on the work of sociologist Martha Beck, who believes modern women are trying to reconcile what is irreconcilable to someone with only 24 hours in a day: women should self-sacrifice and women should pursue their dreams. Mothers feel like they are managing rather than participating in their families, which both spawns feelings of disconnection and fosters a 'learned helplessness' in children and partners. 'I meet mothers who lean into their guilt like it's a security blanket and hold up their self-sacrifice as a badge of honour.' Is there any lesson about our gender that women internalise more than the idea that our selflessness and suffering are somehow redemptive? Is there any realm in which this sacrifice and self-negation is sold as so perpetually rewarding as it is in motherhood? That somehow a woman who gives unconditionally is never depleted because the act itself is so fulfilling. 'On one hand being a martyr is about experiencing pain and destroying yourself for the sake of others,' Lakshmin writes. 'On the other hand it's about seeking glory, and paradoxically, your glory is in your smallness.'

It wasn't until I found myself in a relationship with a man who wanted but didn't need me that I had to admit how much glory I'd found in my smallness, how much value I'd placed on my expertise. I was wholly unprepared to give up a role that I might not have agreed to be cast in but now excelled at. It threw me off balance and made me feel confused and insecure. If he didn't need me, why did he want me? I had to learn how to trust that I was not defined by what I did for my partner but for who I was – a scary proposition for a good listener with an arsenal of recipes but a fairly low reserve of self-esteem. A friend describes a series of relationships in her early 20s with men who had various mental health issues but who had not accessed appropriate help. 'I guess it was definitely nice to feel necessary and useful,' she remembers.

Gemma Hartley says that emotional labour can be 'women's bastion of control' in a world that otherwise limits their power. 'But holding on to control for the sake of control is no way to live,' she writes. 'We're not benefiting from our perfectionism as much as we think we are and neither are men.' Hartley says women create 'an altruistic persona' by allowing themselves to be subsumed by the needs of others. It is humbling to learn the difference between a persona and a personality just as you approach thirty. I can see now how even devoted dishonesty in a relationship can cause harm. I try to be aware of when I am seeking the protection racket of what Professors Susan Fiske and Peter Glick call 'benevolent sexism', in which I gain approval for displaying a quality, like nurturing or comforting, that I am supposedly better at by virtue of my gender. Sexism that endorses positive stereotypes, sexism that we occasionally benefit from, is after all, still sexism.

I would be lying if I said I didn't still need to stop and distinguish between genuine and adequate care, concern and affection and an inextinguishable predisposition to bleed myself dry for someone else. I no longer romanticise this limitless potential to toil for others but nor do I condemn it as a pathetic compulsion to shore up my own worth by giving. Lakshmin writes that releasing oneself from a martyr mentality is like building a muscle which represents your own thoughts, feelings and preferences. 'It's not a luxury; it's a necessity,' she writes. 'And it is a gift only you can give yourself.'

Lately, I find myself conducting a secondary check, just in case. As mainstream feminism pushes for women to catch up and associate themselves with 'masculine' traits like competitiveness, self-interest and self-reliance in pursuit of strength, control and power there can be a blurring of lines in which caring and nurturing, particularly in an unpaid capacity, is seen as a crisis of self-worth, boundary-setting or assertiveness. You can really rebrand any exertion of effort for another person as a failure to 'put yourself first'. @Becky_Lucas89 tweets: 'Girls on the internet talking about self care: "I was drink driving and I hit a cyclist and didn't stop to see if he was okay. I now realise that I don't have to take on that negativity and most importantly, I forgive myself"'.

Mostly though, I just feel in myself and in my friends a genuine desire to have our time and effort valued. I think it is okay to feel indignant and taken for granted. I think it is okay to feel frustrated by a culture that funnelled people into a binary in which they were taught two very different lessons about how to care and communicate. I even think it is okay to feel pessimistic, but I agree with Seresin, who says that heteropessimism can distract from the extent to which heterosexuality is trying to change and in doing so, re-inscribes its worst features. 'Heteropessimism reveals something about the way we can remain secretly attached to the continuity of the very things we (sincerely) decry as toxic, boring, broken,' she writes. 'Faced with the possibility of disappointment, anaesthesia can feel like a balm.' I just don't find resigned heteropessimism soothing anymore. Isn't so much of our frustration rooted in the feeling that things *don't* have to be this way? I don't want to recite the same story about preordained gender relations just so I can be pissed off about them. I want them to change.

Shannon Keating writes that like many lesbians, she has endured drunk straight women who insist their lives would be easier if they were queer. The moping flattens the queer experience into an uncomplicated utopia, devoid of danger or stigma, ignores the ways in which heterotypical gender roles are internalised within same-sex couples and, as Keating argues, it is also just unhelpful to 'pit queerness and straightness against each other'. It is tempting, she writes, for everyone to 'disavow heteronormativity' and its associated institutions altogether. 'But what if we instead used our heteropessimism to encourage each other to reach beyond the bounds of the self – and beyond the bounds of our romantic partnerships and nuclear families – to imagine a better world for us all?'

There is optimism in the reaching, to extend yourself towards the possibility of relationships and families that don't follow the rules you had to. All this premature mothering has helped me to mother myself too, and mum says we're allowed a few sour tweets if we try to harvest something sweet with the people we love most.

6

Legacies

What would we pass on?

Everyone knew which parts of their history they wanted to rhyme, which stories they wanted to rewrite. It was an awareness of how a child could trace you like a stencil, even before you understood the template from which you came. It was not just that secretly drafted but rarely voiced curriculum vitae for the role of 'parent' – it was a risk appraisal. It was a need to stop the past from living in the present, from living in the future. It was a fear of causing harm. It was both self-doubt and self-defence and it surfaced in almost every conversation I had over the nine months. A collection of people living through the positive and negative consequences of actions taken by those in decades past. Perhaps that describes every generation, but millennials are more resentful and armed with an emotional literacy many of our predecessors did not have the latitude to develop before they were parents, or at all. We are all playing clairvoyant, psychoanalyst, weatherperson, theorising about how our genetics, their trauma, their childhoods, our culture might live on in a child.

They were considering not just how the darkest dynamics or brightest memories would shape their families but whether the values, the experiences, the very air they inhaled throughout their childhood might expire out of their own children. What do we want to replicate? Can we sacrifice as readily as our ancestors? Are we destined to repeat their crooked patterns? Does the nervous father raise an anxious kid? Is the neglected daughter destined to smother her own? Or do they overcorrect and inflict an entirely new set of neuroses and painful experiences on their own offspring? How much control do we have over this?

Philip Larkin's legendary poem on the subject concludes with a directive to not reproduce, to stop the cascading misery and let it die out. That is the approach James is taking. He got in touch to talk about how his past had impacted his decision not to have children. 'When I was a lot younger one of my main aspirations and dreams was to be a dad,' the 28-year-old tells me. 'I think because I had a complicated relationship with my dad I wanted to be a really good dad when I was older.' James says his desire for a more present and engaged father left him especially vulnerable to his auntie's partner, who sexually abused him when he was ten. 'He made himself out to be the cool uncle type figure, as is the case with a lot of these predators. They let children in on cool adult secret stuff like he let me watch horror movies,' he says. 'They give this illusion of treating kids as equals and also cast themselves as fulfilling that father role and then they exploit it.' Around this age James began feeling too nauseous to go to school and the doctor could find no discernible cause for the sickness. After he watched a news report about child sexual abuse he realised that he needed to tell his parents. His mother and his grandmother both disclosed to James that they too had in their lifetimes been sexually abused by a family member. 'I think they told me as a means to connect with me . . . I think there are times when my mother blames herself not because she wasn't careful or whatever but because she wasn't a helicopter parent.'

The first time I talk to James he tells me learning of the sexual trauma throughout generations made him feel, however irrationally, that his abuse was in some way inevitable. The second time we speak he is firm that he knows it wasn't fate. An adult made a decision to violate his trust and his body. 'I don't think there is something in my personality that I took on from my mum who took it on from my grandmother, that made me more vulnerable to the abuse.' By the time James was 12 he had been diagnosed with both a major depressive disorder and generalised anxiety disorder. 'For many years afterwards I was very stubborn in not wanting to think about [the abuse],' he says. 'It sat in a box that I would put aside.' This ability, a natural response to trauma, has allowed James to function as safely as possible for many years. 'One of the reasons that I can speak so candidly about this and don't consider myself a closed book is because of this defence mechanism that I developed over time, which is not to say I'm ever unfeeling when I talk about it but I will feel both present and not present,' he says. 'I think that my biggest barrier to truly reckoning with my past is that I can't shake that aspect of being somewhat detached.'

When James was younger and determined to one day be a father, he couldn't know how his trauma would echo through his life. He couldn't know his depression and anxiety would eventually become so much a part of his identity that he now finds it hard to distinguish his symptoms from his personality and his everyday experience of the world. He struggles to describe how his depression and anxiety first manifested because he can't remember a time without them. 'I think [the idea of having kids] was a door that gradually shut for me and now it is for the most part closed,' he says. 'I think when I think about how that yearning for a father figure and the spectre of my father played a role in my life, in throwing me off course in a lot of ways, it scares me and if I were to become a father that would be a burden I would take on and my child would take on.'

It is clear within minutes of speaking to James that he is resilient and perhaps realistic but when I thought of his younger self longing for fatherhood, I hoped he was not being resigned. Both possibilities seem unspeakably unfair. Sophie Mackintosh writes that she envisioned her life free of a child who she might raise badly, one who might inherit her 'unpredictable brain' and who she might fail. 'I had to study the narrative I'd built around myself, the narrative of who I was and what I deserved,' she writes. 'What if having a child wouldn't be a disaster? What if, actually, I was an imperfect person with a lot of love to give?'

At a time before the rights of the child were precious, before corporal punishment was so widely condemned or emotional development so rigorously studied, psychoanalyst Alice Miller's ideas were revolutionary. 'Experience has taught us that we have only one enduring weapon in our struggle against mental illness: the emotional discovery and emotional acceptance of the truth in the individual and unique history of our childhood,' she wrote. Miller upset a longstanding power dynamic in psychology by introducing the perspective of the child and granting people a voice, even if only behind the closed doors of a therapist's office, in their relationship with their parents, in her bestselling 1979 book *The Drama of the Gifted Child*.

She excoriated parents for conventional child-rearing, which she called 'poisonous pedagogy', condemning them for perpetuating cycles of trauma by re-enacting the emotional neglect and violent discipline they had suffered. She told people to reckon with the mistakes made by their parents so they didn't in turn use their child's need for love and care to fulfil their own unmet needs. 'Although the feelings of the abused child have been silenced at the point of origin, that is, in the presence of those who caused the pain, they find their voice when the battered child has children of his own,' she wrote. Children who are not respected for who they are forgo their own emotional needs, adapting themselves to their parents' needs to develop a false self which is unsustainable and is eventually riddled with psychic and somatic illness. 'Our intellect can be deceived, our feelings manipulated, and conceptions confused, and our body tricked with medication,' she wrote. 'But someday our body will present its bill, for it is as incorruptible as a child, who, still whole in spirit, will accept no compromises or excuses, and it will not stop tormenting us until we stop evading the truth.'

You can't outrun your past, she yells from the pages of her books, *it will catch you eventually and haunt your children indefinitely.*

Eight years after her death, Alice Miller's past came for her, just as it had come for her only child, Martin, who claimed she had subjected him to manipulative cruelty and astonishing neglect. In 2018 he published *The True Drama of the Gifted Child*, a devastating riposte to her bestseller in which he researched his mother's horrific personal history and tried to understand why she had perpetrated the emotional abuse she implored others not to in her work. 'I became emotionally a part of my mother's Holocaust experience . . . I became a participant in a history of suffering, even though – or precisely because – it was unknown to me,' Miller wrote. He learned that when his mother was in her early 20s she had to assume a Polish identity, changing her name from Alicjia to Alice, and kill a part of herself in order to survive and free her mother and sister from Warsaw.

Growing up, his mother had told him that his cruel and violent father had the same name as her Gestapo captor but Martin discovered they were one and the same. His mother, a bystander to the violence, was able to disassociate from her surroundings and behave in a way he described as suspicious, short-tempered, insensitive, unreliable, tense and anxious.

As a psychotherapist himself Martin witnessed how war and other hardships could fray the connections a parent had to their child's needs but just as his mother failed to apply her academic propositions to her own son, he could not see her as a product of her context, only the mother who had failed him. Alice Miller was obsessed with how unresolved agony can ricochet through generations and yet she did not, or could not, protect her son from the shrapnel. She was either a perfect case study in her own theory – a parent who refused to face their own history to protect her family – or the ultimate contradiction – a parent who understood her own experiences and still could not stop the harm.

Once we account for physical and emotional abuse – which I agree with Miller, should be broadly defined – can we not release parents from the entire burden of psychic distress? How could a woman who survived the most brutal persecution at the hands of strangers cast parents as the ultimate tyrants? (Miller even in part explained Hitler's atrocities, which claimed many of her family members including her father, by reference to his disciplinarian childhood.) Does becoming aware of your traumatic history actually release you from its lasting consequences or do you just become bitter with rumination? In a passage addressed to his mother, Martin writes: 'Today I am confronted with the paradoxical situation that you harmed me, almost killed me – but thanks to your radical ideas I found a way to save my own life.'

In the end, it was Martin's correction of what he believed was an error in his mother's reasoning that really secured the closest he could come to peace. He learned as a therapist and as a son that when one critically appraises the way they have been raised as a child, it surfaces rage, hatred, mourning, pain and fear about a story you are powerless to edit. Miller believed forgiveness and understanding had a limit when it came to the resentment people have for their parents but nor could his clients 'become children again and start their lives over'. The raging inner child is only comforted by offering oneself as an alternative to their parents and giving themselves the care they were denied, Martin says. Establishing safety and stability you never had in a volatile home, listening to your needs if they were ignored, learning to accept yourself if perfection was demanded of you. It wasn't just tracing his mother's history, exposing himself to each of the horrifying chapters before integrating them, in his own words, into a book about her life, that saved Martin. It was the resultant understanding that he was not an unlovable child worthy of mistreatment but a victim in a story that was being told long before he arrived and, crucially, one he would continue to write.

When Alexa found out she was pregnant with a boy, the flutter of anxiety she felt about having a child began to shake more noticeably inside her, unsettling the expectations of what her growing family might look like. 'I was so convinced that it was a girl and I think that was probably my subconscious telling me so that I wouldn't freak out,' Alexa, now five months pregnant, tells me. She thought to herself, *'Everything you've worried about could actually happen now.'*

Alexa has never thought of herself as maternal – the first baby she will ever hold will be her own – but she felt confident about raising a girl. 'I feel like I know how to teach her to navigate what will come her way and how you can be really strong in the face of all that shit but I don't know how to teach a boy the balance between being strong and being aggressive or being forthright and being too angry. It feels so much harder.' Alexa's fear was not so much about having a son, but about having a son who might one day be a brother, an older brother like Mick. When Alexa started high school, he had a psychotic episode and jumped in front of a train. A few months later, once his bones had mended and he was discharged from hospital with a diagnosis for schizophrenia and depression, the bullying and antagonism he had subjected her to throughout their childhood escalated into constant verbal abuse and intermittent physical violence until she eventually moved out of home, years later. He would barge into her room unannounced, smash her belongings and stand over her, a full foot taller, yelling. 'He would tell me I was an awful person every day of my life,' she says. 'He would call me a "little slut", particularly once I hit puberty.'

Alexa could not stop herself projecting fear after fear onto her foetus: '*What if my kid has really bad mental health issues and can't control them? What if they are a complete arsehole to everyone around them? What if they are just a toxic person?*'

When she first got in touch with me, I made a note next to her name as a potential interviewee: *Alexa, 30s, pregnant, anxious about having a boy as brother schizophrenic.* The note proved wrong. She wasn't preoccupied with the fact that her child's chances of having schizophrenia increased with Mick's diagnosis. In fact, Alexa only ever talked about her brother's disorder as something that might better equip her to recognise warning signs of poor mental health in her own children. She wasn't worried her kid might inherit her sibling's psychotic hallucinations or paranoid delusions; she was worried her kid might subject a sibling to aggression and misogyny. Alexa said she pictured having another child, a girl, and watching these same tensions play out between her imagined children. 'It is irrational but also it's not because my whole life has been dictated by that core relationship and that core relationship has permeated into every other relationship that I have with my family,' she says. 'Every single part of my life has been negatively impacted by it.' It wasn't her son she was most concerned about. It was the possibility of a future daughter.

As Mick took up more of her parents' time and energy, Alexa expected less of them. When she achieved highly at school and then at university they didn't want her to talk about it in case it made her brother insecure. 'I took on the responsibility that I gave myself of always pretending that I was fine and everything was perfect,' she says. Alexa's family home remains out of bounds to her as Mick, who she now hasn't seen in four years, still lives there. The space between Alexa and her father, an already emotionally absent man, has grown while her mother walks on eggshells around Mick's feelings – she asked Alexa to move her wedding date to a day when he would be out of the country so she didn't feel guilty for attending. She suggested perhaps Alexa could write him a letter. 'I said, "No, Mum, I'm not the one that was ever a problem, I'm not the one who beat him up, I'm not the one who abused him every day of his life. If he thinks there is a gap to be bridged he needs to do it."'

As we talk, Alexa's due date, a couple of days shy of her brother's birthday, looms like a prophecy. 'What if he is even born on my brother's birthday?' she says. 'Will Mum even come to the birth or will she not want to leave him on his birthday?'

Before she met her husband, Jack, Alexa says she dated a series of 'absolute losers'. 'I thought that was what all guys were like and it was totally normal for them to be low functioning babies that you had to help through life,' she says.

But Jack took responsibility for himself. He didn't need her to shrink so he could stretch. 'His purpose on this earth is to grow a little human and help them form and he is such a generous and loving and caring person,' she says. 'He will be such a great dad.' When I thank her for her time, she returns the gratitude – 'talking this through has made me realise I really need to process and can't keep avoiding it'. Alexa has for the first time decided to see a mental health professional to support her in facing her dread before the child arrives. Alexa's confidence in her own ability to parent has wavered throughout her pregnancy, which has been plagued with nausea. She arrived at her last ultrasound anxious that her baby might not be getting enough nutrients as she hadn't gained enough weight. 'I was scared I was already giving it a bad start as well as bringing it into a fucked-up family,' she says. The doctor told Alexa her baby was active with a strong heartbeat.

Every day he grows bigger she pictures a new *what if*. 'I am trying to picture what life might be like and it is a good picture. I can imagine loving that kid and I can imagine him loving me. I can imagine having another girl or another boy and them being great together as well and I can see that in my future.'

Whether in the womb or through our relationships, psychologist Mark Wolynn says life sends us forward with something unresolved from the past. 'Traumas do not sleep, even with death, but rather continue to look for the fertile ground of resolution in the children of the following generations,' he writes. Alexa unknowingly practised what Wolynn asks his patients to – she allowed herself to be moved by an image strong enough to overshadow the horror she remembers from her past and that which she has projected into her future. On a neurophysiological level, Alexa is engaging not with her brain's trauma response centre but with her prefrontal cortex, where she can integrate the new image and, Wolynn says, neuroplastic change can occur. 'Our minds have a vast capacity for healing through images whether we're imagining a scene of forgiveness, comfort, or letting go, or simply visualising a loved one, images can profoundly settle into our bodies and sink into our minds,' he writes. Life is rife with suffering but Wolynn believes it is trauma that remains unaddressed and so unresolved that becomes a legacy for our children. 'When the connection remains unconscious we can live imprisoned in feelings and sensations that belong to the past,' he writes. 'However, with our family history in view, the pathways that will set us free become illuminated.'

I want to believe that the hardest moments in life tilt like a series of dominoes falling from one generation into the next, and if we try hard enough we can catch the falling tile before it hits another. I want to believe this even though I know the precursor cell of the egg I developed from was already in my mother's ovaries when she was a five-month old foetus, curled up in my grandmother's womb.

Geneticist Professor Robert Plomin believes DNA is the major systematic force that makes us who we are, and while parents provide 'essential physical and psychological ingredients' for a child's development, the most significant element they give their kids is their genes. Plomin argues that for decades scientists have shown in studies using twins and adoptees that inherited DNA differences account for about half of the differences for all psychological traits, from personality to mental health to cognitive abilities. 'The impact of our experiences is mostly unsystematic, unstable and idiosyncratic – in a word, random,' Plomin writes. 'What look like systematic environmental effects, such as correlations between parenting and children's development, are mostly reflections of genetic influence. In the tumult of daily life, parents mostly respond to genetically driven differences in their children. We read to children who like us to read to them. We go along with their appetites and aptitudes.'

Genetics can't account for everything but research shows how they impact verbal skills, literacy, professional, cognitive and non-cognitive skills. The study of genes in human development usually defines genes as independent predictors of some observable trait (phenotype) or consequence either independently, in the way they influence someone's likelihood to smoke or be successful, or in how they interact with an environmental condition like a stressful life event.

Epigenetics is where nurture and nature meet to offer a different flavour of fatalism on the journey to answer the question of how much I will fuck up any potential offspring. It suggests you can pass on your genes and then adversely impact how those genes are expressed. It is the study of how

216

external modifications to DNA turn genes 'on and off'. For a long time it was supposed that these switches were complete after the embryological period but now there are claims that a person's exposure to environment or experience can actually influence their genes and how they are expressed. A gene responsible for some of the physiological response to stress was turned off in newborn rat pups, who were licked and groomed a lot by their mothers, making them calmer as they developed. One study showed children of prisoners of war were more likely to die young than those of soldiers who were not prisoners. Another showed girls born to women pregnant during a severe famine in the 1940s had an above-average risk of developing schizophrenia and the grandchildren of people who were undernourished at age nine had better mental health.

Studies have shown the descendants of Holocaust survivors have a higher risk of developing post-traumatic stress disorder, depression and anxiety and in 2015 Rachel Yehuda, a professor of psychiatry and neuroscience, published research claiming she had an epigenetic explanation for the inheritance of trauma after studying the genes of Holocaust survivors who had been interned at Nazi concentration camps, forced into hiding during World War II or who had seen or experienced torture. Yehuda was criticised for the small size of her sample and the pre-emptive conclusions she drew before examining the great-grandchildren of these survivors, as a pregnant woman already possesses the DNA of her grandchildren, but her field of genetics is compelling if contested. One participant in Yehuda's controversial study, Josie Glausiusz, whose father survived a concentration camp wrote: 'I was troubled by a question: How does one separate the impact of horrific stories heard in childhood from the influence of epigenetics?' These kinds of distinctions seem impossible. Yehuda herself has said when she first established this clinic for Holocaust survivors, their children would call and report how they experienced the aftermath. 'They talked about feeling traumatised by witnessing the symptoms of their parents. And they talked about the expectations – being traumatised by some of the expectations that the Holocaust had placed on them, such as that they are the reason their parents survived; and, therefore, there was a whole set of things that they would now have to accomplish so that all the people that died would – they could give their lives meaning,' she said.

In her book *Unlike the Heart*, Nicola Redhouse searches for the locus of her postnatal dissolution and whether it was biochemical, hormonal and genetic or whether it was emotional, built in memories and feelings. She wants to know where the sentient part of us that experiences emotion lives, where a 'sorrow of fathers leaving' resides. Redhouse finds studies that conclude perinatal depression has some genetic heritability but wonders if early infant responses to separation could influence our parental attachments. 'My mother feared her mother wouldn't be there; my mother's mothering was fraught with this fear, with attempts to keep me close, perhaps made worse by my father leaving; I in turn embodied a fear of being separated from her, and when I had my own children I fell into a panic both because of the separation, bodily, from them that birth required, and the separation, emotionally, from my mother, that becoming a mother myself required.' Even if Redhouse did locate in herself where the sorrow of fathers leaving slept, could she stop it from waking and disturbing her own children? I think of sorrow moving through time – travelling through molecular scars on our DNA, switching genes on and off, living in the narratives that pass from our grandmother to our granddaughter, fanning out down the branches of our family trees into a complex set of actions and reactions too intricate to be observable.

Taryn knows the most dangerous thing she is likely to pass on through her genes. She found out a few weeks before we spoke. 'You don't realise when you're having sex and trying to have a baby but at some point in the process of becoming a mother you come to this crushing realisation that you're not only creating a life but you're creating a death.'

Taryn and her husband both grew up in small, loving families knitted tightly together into which their baby Louis was woven in 2019. Motherhood felt at first like a psychoactive drug trip. 'You're shimmering with this otherworldly energy and these hormones are just coursing through your body and you feel like you're electric,' she says. 'Three weeks later, exhaustion moves into your body and it just lives beside your bones for months and months and months and months.' In the first year of life with Louis she was bored, exhilarated, overwhelmed, full of love, empty of sleep, heavy with responsibility and foggy-brained. 'I couldn't compute basic conversations and felt like I didn't know how to function but in the midst of that I could be having these really clear profound, almost life-changing realisations,' she says. 'Our relationship and our bond is constant and I feel the tug of him every time we're apart.'

The demands of sleeping and feeding schedules tether new parents to the home in a way that can contract their physical world but Taryn says motherhood expanded a space within her. 'We think of an experience as going somewhere or doing something but the experience of motherhood happens within you,' she says. 'Pregnancy expands you in a physical way. You fill up with this other person and then when they come out through birth they are still you, they just push out and out and you're still encompassed by this person but they are suddenly free in the world.' She begins to cry when she tries to explain what Louis has uncovered inside of her. I feel so moved not only by Taryn's love but by the way she has challenged a foolish misconception I started with while trying to map how we pass things on. I saw that I had believed on some level that a human came to and through parenthood as a fixed and knowable entity. Instead, she had created Louis and he had recreated her. 'He has unlocked this unknown part of me that I was never able to access . . . a tenderness that I really didn't know I had in me,' she says, her voice dense with emotion. 'Even in the really difficult times I know these will be some of the greatest days in my whole life and it is so unusual to recognise that while you're in it.'

Everyone has two copies of the breast cancer gene 1 (BRCA1) and the breast cancer gene 2 (BRCA2), often referred to as tumour suppressor genes. When someone inherits a mutation of these genes they have increased risks of multiple types of cancer, as cells that don't contain the protein can grow out of control and become cancerous. Through genetic testing, Taryn has found out that she inherited a harmful variant of BRCA1 from her mother, who survived an aggressive breast cancer aged forty-two. Around 13 per cent of the general population will develop breast cancer and 1.2 per cent will develop ovarian cancer in their lifetime, while up to 69 per cent of women with a BRCA1 variant will develop breast cancer and up to 44 per cent of them will develop ovarian cancer. 'It was a devastating couple of weeks as I had to come to grips with everything that it meant,' she says. 'They told me that my risk factor of developing breast cancer over the next ten years is 15 per cent but I guess for that 15 per cent it is 100 per cent.'

Taryn has been meeting with oncologists and surgeons to make plans for her eventual double mastectomy and hysterectomy. She knows she can cut out the pieces of her body most vulnerable to cancer but she can't remove the mutation from her own genes. Although the BRCA1 gene does slightly increase a person's risk of prostate cancer, because Louis doesn't have mammary glands or ovaries, if he does have the mutation, it won't impact his life in the way it has Taryn's. Taryn and her partner have discussed their plans to grow their family, going over the risks of passing on the variant – a one in two chance of having a kid with female sex organs, then a one in two chance of her inheriting the mutation. Now that Taryn has confirmed she doesn't already have cancer, they have decided they are going to try for another child.

'I have always known that I want two kids and that doesn't disappear just because I have this genetic flaw,' she says. 'If I do have a daughter and she does inherit this gene, there is a power in the knowledge. It is not something that she would grow up with thinking of a terrible scary life-ruining thing because I'm not going to let it be that for me.'

Taryn and her mother did not know they had the gene until they were tested but Taryn's embryo would be a candidate for a pre-implantation genetic diagnosis (PGD) if she chose to have her child via IVF.

'They create a number of embryos and they can do a needle biopsy and test for BRCA1 and only implant the ones that don't have the mutation,' she says. 'We turned this option over a lot but we have decided against it and we are going to try to conceive naturally.' When she lists her reasons for this, Taryn says she is mostly answering to the hypothetical scrutiny of others. She knows what her values are and feels this decision is in line with them. This is not a diagnosis after all; it is a risk factor. 'The truth is this is a grey area but I know PGD isn't a choice for me because I don't think this optimisation process is necessary with a human being. After all, if my parents took that path I wouldn't exist,' she says, adding that genes are a blueprint for your body, not for your life. 'I like to think that it is not just 50 per cent of my genetics that will shape and determine his whole life but also 100 per cent of my love, devotion, care and respect,' she says. 'I don't think you can decide life isn't worth coming to fruition because of potential future risk. Maybe Louis doesn't have BRCA1 and maybe he will be a rev head and die in a car accident at eighteen.'

When my niece arrived, I knew what I wanted to insulate her from within our extended family in an immediate panic I did not feel when my nephew was born. 'I'm very resentful about it and I'm very angry,' singer Mitski said of the teenage years she spent obsessed with beauty. 'I had so much intelligence and energy and drive, and instead of using that to study more, or instead of pursuing something or going out and learning about or changing the world, I directed all that fire inward, and burned myself up.'

My cousin and I meet up in London for coffee and find ourselves talking about the years we spent on fire. There were two ways to be the belle of our family barbecue: get a new boyfriend or lose a noticeable amount of weight. We remember a 'game' in which an aunt or grandparent would ask 'who is the prettiest girl?' and half a dozen hands would shoot into the air. Whoever was quickest would get to be *her*. It might have been a way of democratising access to the most cherished attribute in our family, beauty, but we knew the game was redundant. It was always obvious who *she* was even once we grew older and the game was retired. The year I stopped eating meat and started exercising too much, I was she. My cousin and I recite like hymns the lessons we learned about which bits of our bodies were meant to be smallest (arms especially) and if you didn't have the self-discipline, at least cover them up. How did we both know the same words?

If I have a child, my body is where it will first find a home. I wondered how a habitat that spent so long trying to contract could be hospitable to new life. It took years for me to put out the flames: to stop exercising in a way that was obsessive, to strip food of morality, to see my body for what it was – a heart mercifully beating, legs generously carrying, hands helpfully typing – and not what it wasn't, to value myself the same way I had always valued others: for what was inside. Now, when I sense the burning, I imagine repeating my internal dialogue word for word to my niece and I stamp until only embers remain.

In Meg Mason's novel *Sorrow and Bliss*, a woman yells at a child who isn't hers in a change room. Childfree Martha asks her sister, the mother of three small children, whether when you have kids you become better at tolerating cruelty in the world, especially against children. Ingrid responds no. 'It makes it worse because as soon as you're a mother, you realise every child was a baby five seconds ago, and how could anyone shout at a baby? But then, you shout at your own and if you can do that, you must be a terrible person. Before you had kids, you were allowed to think you were a good person so then you secretly resent them for making you realise you're actually a monster.'

In a letter to his mother, who was at times abusive, Ocean Vuong remembers that while pruning green beans over the sink, she suddenly said, 'I'm not a monster. I'm a mother.' He told her at the time that she was not a monster, but now wishes he had instead told her it wasn't the worst thing to be. 'From the Latin root *monstrum*, a divine messenger of catastrophe, then adapted by the Old French to mean an animal of myriad origins: centaur, griffin, satyr,' he writes in the letter, published in the *New Yorker*. 'To be a monster is to be a hybrid signal, a lighthouse: both shelter and warning at once.'

The chimera, a fire-breathing monster made up of goat, lion and snake, forewarned rain, lightning and thunder in Greek mythology. A genetic chimera is a single organism composed of cells with more than one distinct genotype and fetomaternal microchimerism involves cells that originate from a foetus lingering in the mother. We take our mother's cells and she takes some of ours. It happens in pregnancy whether it ends in miscarriage, abortion or a live birth. These cells make mothers weaker and stronger – they can promote tissue repair and improve her immune system but they can also wreak havoc, catalysing autoimmune reactions. 'It's not only us,' cancer researcher Sami B Kanaan told the *Boston Globe*. 'It's us, plus our mothers, plus our children if we have them, that are living with us.'

'Millennial parents are more aware of things within themselves that don't feel good, places that feel empty that they want to feel sturdier,' clinical psychologist Dr Becky Kennedy told the *New York Times*. 'These are parents dedicated to raising kids who feel solid and confident while also trying to heal *themselves*.' When asked whether happiness was the goal of parenting, Kennedy responded: 'No. Anybody who had a childhood in which happiness was the goal would be predestined for a lifetime of anxiety – life is full of distress!' She said parents should not be aiming to extinguish hard feelings in their children but should be letting them know they are not alone in these feelings and that they can be dimmed.

In *The Origins of You: How Childhood Shapes Later Life*, four psychologists explain their 40 years of research involving more than 4,000 children. They map how family experience and experiences beyond the family shaped who they became later in life by picking apart how children think, feel and behave as they move from childhood, through adolescence and into adulthood. Research has repeatedly shown that parents who mistreated their children were disproportionately likely to have been mistreated themselves but the authors say there are 'serious problems' with the collection of this data as it relies on memory, a fallible value. They instead give more credence to evidence, tricky and time-consuming to obtain (over generations), that links actual assessments of parenting experienced in childhood with the parenting that the child, now grown up, provides for their own offspring. This research showed the way mothers parent is influenced by their experiences in their families growing up but there was no such evidence of intergenerational transmission from fathers. In trying to describe the complexity of all that is unknown, the experts describe the science of human development as similar to meteorology. Just as studying the weather and climate must account for multiple and often competing factors and forces, human development involves many elements – emotion, cognition, behaviour, neuroscience, genetics, physiology – that interact in complex ways over time and space.

The idea that success relies on securing a number of factors while failure can hinge on a single deficiency is sometimes referred to as the Anna Karenina principle, after Tolstoy's famous opening: 'Happy families are all alike; each unhappy family is unhappy in its own way.' Even the most rational person can't accurately appraise the positive or negative impacts their parents had on their development. I know my parents smoked through all four of their pregnancies. The advertised harms of this had changed rapidly over those decades – my mother was allowed to smoke on the maternity ward after she had her first child in 1976 but by the time she had her last child, me, in 1992 she had to go out onto the hospital balcony to light up, which she did. And yet I harbour no judgement, resentment or concern about the documented effect this has on a foetus's brain or lung development. I feel nothing and so it means nothing to me. I never begrudge rain until I'm inconvenienced by it.

We can know ourselves, we can know our family histories, we can know that children need to be safe, loved, regarded and respected. We can't know the unique ways in which a child of ours might suffer or inflict suffering on others, including their parents, any more than we can predict the weather. Harsh physical punishment, for example, can 'and often does' foster aggression in a child, the experts write, but whether it does depends on a range of environmental factors including whether they have a sensitive nervous system or whether their other parent's love and affection can temper the impact of the abuse. Human development, like meteorology, is probabilistic, not deterministic. 'Whether a storm will turn into a hurricane may depend not only on its characteristics but also on whether air pressure in another locale will increase the time the hurricane spends out at sea, picking up moisture, before making landfall,' *The Origins of You* researchers wrote.

A probability is not an outcome, history is not a forecast. In imagining what I might pass on to a child genetically or emotionally I saw how quickly I could become that person pointing at their phone screen, insisting it is currently raining because there is a cloud emoji for the day, as the sun sparkles outside my window. A realisation kept recurring.

It would surface late in each conversation and later still in the one I was having with myself. Beyond this fear of what we might pass on, behind the self-deprecating jokes about how dysfunctional we were, was an obscured terror about what we might *not* pass on. We were all uneasy and ill-prepared for how different our children might be.

Researchers found people who watched post-apocalyptic movies coped better with the pandemic as they had 'mentally rehearsed' an analogous scenario. There was a sense of preparedness in the anxiety about precisely how you might mess up your kids. Adversity can cripple our capacity for trust, joy, security, stability and hope but it connects us to others who have suffered in similar ways. Gender is a blunt way to parse this feeling because every woman I know is so acutely aware of what they do not want the next generation of women to experience and so determined to not be complicit in repeating it. I could feel it in my self-censorship around my niece. I could feel it in Alexa's initial panic about not feeling up to raising a boy who might embody the sharpest edges of masculinity. Many women I know admit they have a preference for a girl. One recently expressed it in a way that made me instantly nauseous: 'I guess maybe it seems easier to raise a victim than a perpe-trator.' The statement was jarring, but more uncomfortable was that I instantly knew what she meant. I worried that meant 'I don't want parenthood if it is hard'. I worried that meant 'I don't want a child that isn't a replica of me'. I worried that meant 'I can only empathise with suffering that looks like mine'. But when I sat with it, it just felt like ineptitude. I understood the lack of faith in your ability to best parent children who are nothing like us, who do not suffer or find joy in the ways that we do, who might live in a way that is antithetical to our values, who might cause harm to others.

My friend and I send voice memos. 'I think it is wanting to know you could love a child unconditionally even if they're different from you. I don't think people are like, "Oh no! What if my teenager has an anti-democratic opposition to equality?" I think they're more like, "What if they're a little brat, like, worryingly so, and I couldn't connect with them or make them feel connected?"' I ramble, feeling stupid.

'I just think most people's kids suck and most parents make mistakes,' she says in her response.

When Sarah Sentilles wrote about trying to adopt a baby through foster care, she said people told her, 'but you never know what you're going to get'. They also said this to her friend who was considering adoption, whose two-year-old son died of a fatal genetic disease. 'Belief in biology runs deep,' Sentilles wrote. 'Fear of the unknown, of the unrelated, runs deeper.' Your children might indeed inherit something of your mental health, disposition, tendencies or experiences but they might not catch any of it. I have little but love in common with my parents.

'Though many of us take pride in how different we are from our parents, we are endlessly sad at how different our children are from us,' writes Andrew Solomon, who spent a decade interviewing more than 300 families with children who had what he calls 'horizontal' identities like deafness, schizophrenia or prodigal intelligence. Unlike vertical identities, attributes and values seamlessly passed through genetics or shared cultural norms, horizontal identities were often, at least at first, an affront, treated as flaws. Solomon documented in detail the struggles and successes of parents trying to integrate their child's difference into their family. He began his book trying to forgive his parents, who accepted his dyslexia but struggled at first to celebrate his sexuality, and ended it by becoming a parent, realising his research about parenting was also a means to subdue his own anxieties about impending fatherhood. Solomon described a positive connection to his parents tainted with a despair at his family dynamics where he found it hard to distinguish between their emotions and his own. He wanted to understand why he had suffered so much in his childhood and to separate what was attributable to himself, what he could blame his parents for and what he found reflected in the society around him. 'I had been consumed by being a son; recently emerged from that whale's mouth, I was afraid to be swallowed by being a father. I was also afraid of becoming the oppressor of a child who was different from me, as I had at times felt oppressed.'

Beyond what I fear I might replicate, beyond what I fear I might find alien, is a fear of failure. It is not only the strangeness but the modern expectation that we should perfectly handle the strangeness that makes me feel nervous about my potential as a parent. Good parents are now more than ever defined by how accepting they are and less by historical measures of raising obedient and well-behaved children, writes philosopher Agnes Callard. She believes there has been a 'deep tectonic shift' in parenting that leaves parents feeling like failures despite spending more time with their children than previous generations. 'Parents have always justified themselves with reference to the future – you'll thank me later! – and parents have always aimed at the happiness of their child,' she writes. '[But] at no point in the past was the parental inability to accept that which strikes them as antithetical to their basic understanding of what is true and what is good perceived as a potential failure by the parents' own standards . . . What's radically new is not, at heart, how concerned or permissive we've become, but how fully we have given over to our children the job of defining "happiness".'

Parents can no longer rely on values of the past to be handed on or the traditional standards on which children are to be assessed, as they are no longer trying to give their children some version of their lives but instead this unknown life based on an unknown future. 'Like all forms of freedom, acceptance parenting makes life more, and not less, stressful. If the parent is demoted from wise authority figure to tentative spokesperson for the child's future self, childhood and child-rearing become a nerve-wracking quest to find one's own footing,' she writes. 'The problem here is not my fear of employing discipline, or my inclination to micromanage. The problem is ignorance. Unlike my forebears, I don't know the things I need to know in order to be a good parent, and none of the people telling me to calm down know those things either. The only one who might know, my grown child, doesn't yet exist.'

Jacqueline Rose worries about the expectation to provide a love that can never fray or falter. 'Expecting mothers to be perfect is, of course, not unrelated to the drive to perfection of the so-called whole world – a world that must be flawless – in her baby,' she writes. 'Or to put it another way, if you're asking mothers to be perfect, why wouldn't they pass that impossible demand on to their child?'

Unlike many of the people I spoke to, Taryn is not taming ghosts hovering above her family but is facing a current and corporeal reality in which she has data to evaluate a real genetic risk. There is so much in between the medical risks and the reality of her family's future. So instead of forecasting, she is already trying to have a looser grasp on what will come, letting each projection and possibility run through her fingers while she asks herself the questions she knows she needs to answer first before having another child. 'What are my values? What are my fears? What are my tendencies? What is my personality? What is my genetic predisposition? What is anxiety and what is real? What are the points in my life that I know "this is legitimate"?' she asks. 'It is when I have my son sitting on my lap. It is real, no matter how loud my anxiety is.'

Years before I carried in my pocket the ability to prevent getting lost, obliterate uncertainty or know instantly the weather forecast in real-time, before spontaneity was a thing you planned to do tomorrow, it began sprinkling while my cousin and I were swimming in the ocean. We were almost at womanhood and though we had the kindling for the fire we would later subject our bodies to, we were still displaying them with pride – leaping across the netball court, practising handstands, performing choreographed dances for our families. We looked back to the beach, now empty of men, empty of anyone, and pulled off our bikinis, laughing and cawing like seagulls as the sky cracked further open and poured down on us. A flash of lightning illuminated my cousin's bum as she mooned the clouds, diving under a wave before it crashed. Later, we carried our sopping wet towels home, shivering, yapping about how brave we were.

I thought my nostalgia for that day was a yearning for a time before my relationship with my body became complicated by rules, a time when I could just be a nude comet racing on the waves, my hips grazing the sand as I hit the shore. Now I miss something else about that moment – the ability to let go, to let life happen to me, to find joy in the unexpected, meeting it arms wide open, fully exposed. I can't remember the last time I swam in the rain. I only go to the beach between October and May, and only if I've checked that it is going to be above 24 degrees.

7

Fertility

This shard of plastic releasing progestin is my prayer, my promise, my postponement. The wishbone stationed in my uterus has given me time. Time to love and leave the wrong-at-the-right-time people, the right-at-the-wrong-time people, the wrong-at-the-wrong time people with nothing created together but fond or faulty memories and flimsy flat-packed furniture. Time to understand that you could feast on only friendship until the end of time. Time to learn together, women talking into the night, saving even more time by sharing the signs – if he is possessive, if he bares his teeth at your strength, if he tells you what to wear, who you can see and how to eat. 'Gina, I'm telling you, if he polices your choices and refuses to look at you from the neck up when you have your hair tied back because you look prettier with it down, it is time, it is time, it is time.' Time to make an escape plan. Time to know that if someone wants forever and you only want today, you need to let them give all of their tomorrows to someone else. Time to study, time to read, time to be self-sufficient, time to work, time to be itinerant, living with stranger after stranger until you are familiar with yourself. Time to know you can be alone. Time to spend the most indulgent nine months of your life figuring out whether you want to be a mother.

We insert fragments of polyethylene into our arms and through our cervixes that make us cramp, we take injections and swallow pills until our heads and breasts ache, until our emotions, our weight, our skin and our libido feel beyond our control. Contraception is ultimately safer than pregnancy and childbirth but our bodies pay a price. For years I was on a pill that has killed multiple women because it increases your risk of blood clots. Soon after I got my intrauterine device (IUD), which has been linked to a higher risk of ovarian cysts, ectopic pregnancy and intracranial hyper-tension, I wrote about a trial for a male contraceptive that was cut short because participants were pulling out. The men in the study found the side effects too burdensome.

My friends and I talk about where we would be without contraception. If we bore children before we knew whether we wanted to, before we had found in ourselves the knowl-edge or esteem we needed to survive. Women who were figuring out who they are, permanently tied to men who were doing the same. We shudder, we shiver with relief. We marvel at how much we have changed in more than a decade, as if sure we have arrived at who we are. As if the sun and rain won't force us to grow anymore. As if the 17-year-old who marched into the GP for a prescription for the pill didn't think she was fully grown. As if I haven't wondered whether my ideas and values will shift by the time this even makes it to print.

A friend goes off her contraception to try to conceive. I can't imagine what that would feel like, to withdraw your weapon after years of defending, to dream of what would have been a nightmare at a different time, with a different person. I wonder what all this time has done to my imagination, whether all the years have convinced me of my ability to control my own fertility. Each year I have achieved the desired outcome: not pregnant. I wonder whether all this time has allowed me to dawdle, refusing to engage in the maths, the blunt ranking of what and when I would sacrifice physically, emotionally and financially for a child.

The asking, the wanting, the choosing, the trying. Are these single steps that come in a universal sequence? What does each process do to the other? How long should we allow for each one? For years I interviewed women who did everything they could to prevent pregnancies and still ended up pregnant. I had almost forgotten that it can be a deliberate choice and for many people one they need to choose again and again before they have a child that is theirs, whether by blood or law. I found people who showed me how 'Should we?' can come before and after and before and after and before and after 'Can we?', the two questions charging and depleting each other.

237

Contraception has long protected my 'no' to mother-hood by preventing pregnancy but it has also guarded my 'yes' without my knowing by alleviating endometriosis, a condition that will likely impact my fertility. My IUD has not only shielded me from much of the bleeding and debilitating pain that comes with endometriosis by disrupting my menstruation and ovulation but it can slow the growth of endometrial tissue and prevent new tissue from forming. Tissue similar to that which lines the inside of the uterus will continue to embroider itself beyond it, across my ovaries, along my fallopian tubes or around pelvic organs, possibly scarring them. It could affect my egg quality, it could disrupt egg implantation, it could cause my immune system to attack an embryo. It might raise my chances of miscarriage and stillbirth.

Before I was born, when my mother wasn't much older than I am now, she miscarried. She kept the lost pregnancy in the freezer for a few weeks. I think about this a lot. I think about how her life caring for three young children would have gone on at a rapid pace while her grief was frozen still. When I imagine the moment she decided to take it out of the freezer, I am sure that I have never experienced real loss. I don't know if I could open myself up to it even once. I can't imagine deciding that I might want to conceive, finding out I can and then the grief, then the loss, then, maybe, nothing.

Grace and her husband always wanted children but life – study, work, family, health – got in the way, as did a series of medical professionals who told Grace she needed to lose weight before trying. When she was 39, Grace found a clinic that was happy to accept her as a patient. She fell pregnant on the first IVF cycle. 'We just couldn't believe that we had been so lucky,' Grace says. 'Until it happened, I hadn't realised this is what I had been waiting for so long.' She knew immediately how she wanted to raise her child. 'I knew I didn't want to necessarily enforce the way I live my life but just to truly see them for who they are,' she says. 'There was something so powerful about thinking about raising them with unconditional love.' Grace said there was some cultural pressure to have children but her parents, who had always been gentle with her, were thrilled about the pregnancy. The global pandemic was just beginning but Grace felt invincible. 'It felt really blissful,' she says. 'It was one of the few times that I have felt completely content and at peace.'

At ten weeks, she experienced light bleeding, at 12 weeks she was told there had been delayed growth, at 14 weeks her obstetrician told Grace there was not enough amniotic fluid and her placenta was not looking like it should this far into a pregnancy. By 15 weeks she was referred to a maternal-foetal medicine specialist who told her, 'this is not going to be a good outcome' but that 'where there is a heartbeat, there is hope'. She was told her only option was to induce the pregnancy and give birth. 'I couldn't decide to induce and watch my baby die.' So Grace waited. Week after week passed. 'I always thought I could be pragmatic when it came to things like this and that I could look at the facts, take on the advice and make a decision but when they were asking me to bring forward the labour and be induced . . . I just said, "I need to know more. I need time."'

For the next ten weeks, Grace underwent devastating scan after devastating scan. At 23 weeks, they told her that her membranes had ruptured and there was now no amniotic fluid around the foetus. At 26 weeks, her case was presented to a roundtable of doctors and she was told they unanimously agreed there was no hope. But there was a heartbeat. 'And where there was a heartbeat, there was hope,' Grace repeated. She played 'Here Comes The Sun' by Nina Simone during IVF, she played it during pregnancy and she played it when she went into spontaneous labour at 28 weeks and had to give birth once her baby's heartbeat had stopped. 'I wasn't scared,' she says. 'I just really wanted to meet my baby even though I knew she wasn't going to be alive.' Orla was placed in Grace's arms. 'She was so tiny but so beautifully formed,' she says, sobbing. 'Everything felt right. The three of us together even though she wasn't moving.' It wasn't just sadness, Grace insists. 'In any relationship where there is love there is also grief.' When Grace arrived home there were bunches of flowers sent from friends. They were all white, the colour of sympathy. 'I don't want people to be sorry for our loss . . . I don't know how to say it was joyful without looking like I have lost my marbles.' Now she buys brightly coloured flowers every week in honour of her daughter.

Grace has done two more cycles of IVF. 'I want another baby,' she says. 'I am happy to keep going until my body says "no more".'

When Sally and Jay began trying to have a baby, they expected to conceive quickly. 'I was 29 and I was ready,' Sally remembers. By the time we speak they have together endured ten rounds of IVF and four miscarriages over five years. It is hard to believe, watching them turning to each other and then to me, openly explaining the toll of the hope and exhaustion, that there were first times for everything – the first time they realised they might not be able to conceive easily, the first time they borrowed $10,000 for the first round of IVF, the first pregnancy loss, the first wave of judgement from their loved ones. 'I remember being by myself and up in stirrups, waiting for them to do this for me and I was just weeping because I knew this wasn't going to work and I was by myself under these bright lights and you're so open and vulnerable and they are sticking things up inside of you and it's all a waste,' Sally says. She can't accept that she might not have kids. Not at 33 years old, not with so many eggs, not when they haven't been able to find a reason why. Jay has a low sperm count but it does not explain why IVF has been unsuccessful. 'It should be working and it's not, which is so hard to reconcile with. How do you stop when you don't know what is wrong?' The couple are now considering donor eggs or surrogacy. 'If we end up in a situation where we stop trying and we don't end up with kids, it will be that we have found a way to live our lives without kids rather than consciously deciding we don't need to have children,' Jay says.

They have learned how much they didn't know about the process: 'How it often doesn't work, how you can pay $10,000 and end up with nothing or end up in the situation we are in now and pay $100,000 and end up with absolutely nothing.'

The cost of these procedures makes them completely inaccessible for many people and only accessible to a point for some people. I can't help but consider the economics of delay. Are the same people delaying starting a family until they achieve financial stability in fact increasing their chance of future debt through IVF? Is this kind of consideration unthinkable to anyone but the ambivalent? In between the numbers, Sally and Jay have learned how they can both express grief differently and still want a child just as much as each other. Early on, Sally responded with open expressions of sadness and Jay did not. 'I just completely shut down so I wouldn't have to deal with it and that was my way of trying to cope,' he says. Now they are together fighting for the family they want. 'I don't want to think about a life without children because that is so deeply not my choice,' Sally says. 'We have really shown ourselves that we really do want a child somehow.'

Sally and Jay seem to chart their position in the world by proximity to their life as parents. They're living in the almost. 'We have been in a holding pattern for like five years, not living our full lives,' she says, looking at him, both of them in tender suspension, orbiting the life they want, waiting to descend.

Alexandra Kimball writes that her grief about not conceiving made her feel like a stack of multiple identical women, 'a chain of paper dolls that had been cut but not yet pulled apart'. Each of these dolls were living separate lives, some still childless, some as mothers. 'It's less about the loss of a potential child than it is about the endless possibility that there may yet be an actual child,' she writes.

Sally talks about the idea of the life she wants to lead and she looks momentarily dazed before she says softly, 'I get so lost thinking about all that stuff.' Jay says they have faced judgement. 'It's like it is your fault for not being able to do it and you should just give up on the process and adopt.' When Sally had a termination for a pregnancy in her early 20s, she felt there was room in her friendships and in feminism to talk about it without shame but with infertility, she has found the smallest space, on a short lease. 'When I had my abortion I belonged somewhere and I had a place to understand that time . . . but this,' she sighs. 'This, the biggest experience of my life and the most traumatic, is totally absent from that discourse and it makes me pretty fucking furious.'

When I reported on stillbirth or miscarriage I would receive messages or tweets about my hypocrisy in interviewing people about these tragedies and also interviewing people about the lack of abortion access in Australia. I don't see a contradiction. I just see the reality – up to one in four women in this country will terminate a pregnancy, up to one in five pregnancies end in miscarriage and one in every 135 pregnancies that reach 20 weeks will end with a stillbirth. Hundreds of thousands of people will in their lifetime have a pregnancy that is planned and a pregnancy that isn't. They will make choices again and again about what is right for them and their children. They will conceive, they will grieve. They will sit over toilets sobbing in pain as a pregnancy leaves them, whether spontaneously or with the help of two pills. Our bodies have long made space for complex truths.

Sally says while her favourite popular feminists are able to speak about abortion, the division of domestic labour, sexual politics, harassment and violence and the workforce, they don't touch infertility. Feminism as we know it, drenched with a consumerist focus on choice, has done much to remove stigma around choosing contraception and abortion and little to support the plight of the infertile. This is partly because of the silhouette around which popular feminism still organises – a privileged figure wanting to prevent or discontinue pregnancies and so, as Kimball writes, resolving infertility is left by feminism to 'passive faith' rather than political or material action. 'In the language of hope, infertility is not a matter between women and the world, but one woman and fate.'

When I think about every part of their bodies, every moment of their time, every reserve of the energy this couple has given to the administrative, financial and emotional ordeal of trying to start a family I understand why they want their loved ones to understand these numbers are a catalogue of trying, not failing. We talk about the study that found the anxiety and depression levels of infertile women were equal to those living with cancer. Sally and Jay want recognition of this effort in a way feminism has failed to account for and, in doing so, reproduces the most ancient tropes of motherhood as natural and easy. 'When maternity is the subject of effort, labour and desire, it is unnatural and what does not happen naturally must be constructed,' Kimball writes, summarising where feminism has failed. 'And what is constructed, especially under patriarchy, must be less valid.'

In Australia you can only get a rebate for fertility treatment if there is a 'medical problem' – same-sex couples and single women are still categorised as 'socially' rather than 'medically' infertile and are locked out of subsidies. The persistent ideal of the young, fertile, cis-gendered, hetero-sexual couple who are ready and determined to conceive in their 20s neglects the reality of family-making for most people and in doing so, erases their love and labour. Parenthood can begin long before you have a child.

Steve and his wife stopped using contraception on their honeymoon. 'I thought in a couple of months we'd be pregnant,' he says. 'Clearly high school biology had failed me because I had so much to learn about the physiology of fertility periods.' The next year they fell pregnant and miscarried at six weeks. A few months later came another pregnancy followed by another miscarriage.

'We were both suffering alone and it placed a lot of strain on our relationship because we didn't know how to talk about it and it was so uncommon to talk about it that it reinforced this feeling that we were doing something wrong,' he says. 'I didn't feel that I deserved to have feelings about it because I wasn't having the miscarriage.' Steve says the entire process challenged his 'masculinity' or the ideas he had absorbed about maintaining power and control over a situation. 'I felt like I hadn't protected our unborn kid.' When they didn't conceive he was anxious it was his fault, that he was not 'man enough' to produce a child, despite the fact that a third of fertility problems originate with a male.

Ovulation cycle after ovulation cycle passed without another positive pregnancy test. They decided to try IVF. They had appointments, underwent tests and collected samples. Steve's wife began injecting herself with fertility medication and then a trigger injection when the time was right to collect her eggs. Then came the fertilisation, embryo development and embryo transfer and, eventually, a chemical pregnancy – a very early miscarriage that happens when an egg is fertilised but doesn't fully implant in the uterus.

When they went through IVF he felt he had no agency, that he was a passive patient in a medical process defined by chance. He wasn't sure who to talk to. 'It made me reflect on who I actually talk to and what my friends and

I actually speak about and how seemingly superficial a lot of guy friendships actually are, which is kind of sad,' he says. Eventually, he went to a psychologist and one by one spoke to his female colleagues, many of whom had themselves suffered pregnancy loss. 'It was really nice to have people to talk to about it,' he says. 'We spend so much time talking about the end result of a pregnancy, a child, but don't talk about the struggle which gets you to that point where you have a baby in your hands if you're lucky to even get one . . . I think if I knew it was common and if I knew it might take longer it would have helped when things didn't go right.' When they fell pregnant again, a question mark punctuated every test and trimester until their son was in their arms.

Reporting on reproductive healthcare has overexposed me to all that can go wrong inside a uterus – interviewing women who have had devastating foetal anomalies, struggled to conceive, had stillbirths and miscarriages. It has all compromised the joy I feel when someone tells me they are pregnant, especially before 20 weeks. It is harder to gauge how rational that fear of grief and struggle is when people I know start experiencing miscarriage and infertility. I would never have started a conversation with Steve about pregnancy loss. I felt nervous about public announcements, status updates excitedly posted, cots pre-emptively purchased. But in mid-2019 I was scrolling through Instagram and saw Nayuka, a Gunai, Gunditjmara Wiradjuri and Yorta Yorta writer, and their partner's smiling faces, squinting into the sunlight as they announced they were eight weeks pregnant with twins. 'Was reticent about sharing because apparently you're not meant to share until second trimester but the only reason for that is because we are scared to talk about death and grief and that seems really white to me and in any case if we're grieving we would want our community to be there for us anyways,' Nayuka wrote. It challenged my instinct to protect people by wishing their joy stays private so their pain might too. It made me question my participation in an online practice of sharing that was really a curation of withholding – in this case, tragedy and the fragility of the human body. It reminded me that I usually only found out about people's miscarriages well after the fact. It made me ask questions about hoping alone. For the record, Nayuka does not think hope for the world is a prerequisite for creating or sustaining a family. 'I am not particularly hopeful on a grand scale . . . I come from a people who like three members of the clan survived a massacre so I don't think anyone should or shouldn't feel pressure to have children but for me the fact that the world is so brutal and still so racist and still a colonial mess that isn't enough for me to not have kids because not having kids would be completion, in a way, of genocide,' they say.

When Nayuka and their partner began trying to conceive, they went to an IVF clinic. 'They're driven by profit but they're also driven by risk so they evaluate you based on risk which no other population [trying to conceive] has to go through,' they say. 'You are subjected to a psych evaluation as a couple, individual and group and there was a police check. I was like "my family, my great-grandmother was taken, my grandfather was taken, I'm going to have Black kids, the less state intervention the better why would I opt into it if I didn't have to?"'

Instead, the couple found a sperm donor and created a family at home. They now have a pair of happy, healthy twins. 'I want people to know that you can do things without clinics and without state intervention,' Nayuka says. Their donor was Enoch, an Indigenous and Polynesian screenwriter. 'The whole idea of weighing up pros and cons for this felt really white,' Enoch describes on a podcast about their donation as a favour for their queer Black family. 'Sometimes when family need help, you just do and when asked for sperm, you bet I came.' The dithering about whether it is ethical to bring children into the world – 'over-population, fires, COVID, police just can't stop killing Black people' – feel to Enoch like 'white projections of guilt'.

'I can't help that feel that instead of policing Black bodies and what they should be doing with them, or whether they should be making kids, maybe we should start by telling the state to stop stealing kids or locking kids up,' Enoch says. 'Now I can't wait to see two young people experience play, community and the ultimate beauty of what it means to be Black.'

I ask Nayuka, 'The way you did things by not involving a corporation . . . and I don't want to romanticise it but did it feel like you were kind of solving fertility via community?'

'No, that isn't romanticising it at all. That is how we feel.' Nayuka says another queer friend explained the insemination method. 'I have been able to pass that queer transmission of knowledge on to other people and there is something really nice about that,' they say. 'I think about pre-colonial times and what families were and what mother-hood was. We didn't have this nuclear family and this idea that it was just a mum and a dad and I don't see how a single woman today asking for sperm and then that kid being raised in the community is really any different to pre-colonial stuff.' We talk about what is considered natural.

Kimball writes that it is clear whose pregnancies fall on the side of the arbitrary street where judgement lives despite the fact that the line between technology and nature has long blurred when it comes to making families. 'Is the pregnancy of a couple who are together because they met online, who are both alive because of a lifetime of vaccines and antibiotics, that was bookended by hormonal contraception and elective sterilisation, and which will be monitored by ultrasound and amniocentesis, really more "natural" than say, that of an infertile couple who uses IVF to select a male embryo or a lesbian couple who uses donor sperm?'

When I mentioned to my family what I was setting out to do over nine months, the conversation turned into one about how women were choosing not to have children. Someone described it as an 'interference', saying that by delaying pregnancy (presumably they knew through long-term contraception and not holy abstinence), women like me

250

were meddling with our natural destiny as hatcheries. Yet I knew that if I had then used assisted reproductive technology to reproduce they would pass the fruit of my loins around, cooing and pinching, no accusations of intervention.

Rob has always imagined himself as a dad. 'Even though I'm gay it had never really occurred to me to consider a life without kids,' he says. 'I guess I had never really thought about the mechanics of having kids myself until we were engaged. We thought *"Oh we will adopt"* or *"Oh we'll have a surrogate".*'

The couple decided to go down the altruistic surrogacy route and chose Canada, where there is an established surrogacy network and where they wouldn't be taking a place in a small pool of potential surrogates and egg donors in Australia from someone who couldn't afford to go overseas. 'Everyone told us this would be hard and they'd say, "You have to understand things will go wrong, you'll get false leads, you'll begin the process with a potential surrogate and egg donor and she will pull out for various reasons" and I thought, *"Yeah but that won't happen to us, we'll be fine".* That is my natural disposition,' he says. 'Then the pandemic hit and things changed.' Their plans to travel to Canada, go through altruistic surrogacy and start their family were grounded along with international flights. Rob is 32 and his husband is 37 and felt like the delays were pushing him into an 'older dad' bracket.

When Rob received an email from the fertility clinic checking in on them in the first big wave of Australia's COVID-19 cases, he found himself poised above his keyboard, stiff with emotion, an anxious shell hardening for a moment around the soft tissue of what he wanted most. He discussed with his partner whether they wanted to continue trying. 'He has less appetite for the ups and downs and didn't want to go through these false starts and heartbreak and that was quite confronting for me because I had never considered life without kids,' he says. 'For the first time I had to assess what my purpose in life was if not kids and whether that was something I was comfortable or happy with.' Rob sees parenthood as the likely end of his full-time career and he is okay with that. 'I get a lot more fulfilment spending a day with a child and going to the park and reading them books than I do at work and I didn't really realise that until I was confronted with the possibility of not having children,' he says. 'It was the realisation that none of it really matters that much and that my career has provided me with a stable enough financial life to have children more than it has anything else.' He couldn't imagine himself building an entire life around work and even the perks – more disposable income, travel, freedom – didn't feel like they would sustain him into his old age. They decided to keep trying while in Australia.

Rob and his husband are two high earners with a company benefit that covers a chunk of the surrogacy costs but still they had flights, accommodation and legal fees to pay for and then, in the midst of a pandemic, they needed to organise getting a refrigerated box through customs into the country and their sperm back out through customs. Every step of the process was followed up by an invoice but Rob says the biggest drain was not financial but administrative. Making a family takes a lot of emails. They have a Canadian fertility clinic, a surrogacy agency, a lawyer in Australia, a lawyer in Canada and a lawyer in the United Kingdom, where Rob's husband hails from. 'The mental space taken up by the logistics alone is more than I ever imagined and it is exhausting,' he says. 'The surrogacy community is made up of people who have been through the process themselves and are trying to make it easier for others but it can feel like an army of people are involved in a personal decision.'

Every email, every bill, every sample of bodily fluid is a reminder of the extra burden they have to undertake to start a family. 'I think when we get through this and if we are able to have a baby . . . not to suggest that we are going to love our child any more than a straight couple would but I think there would be an appreciation of the amount of work and sacrifice that goes into it that makes it if not sweeter or better but . . . something.' Rob pauses, trying to be diplomatic. 'There have been a number of barriers placed in our way by all sorts of factors and it would be easier to stop and a lot of intended parents would. I guess what I am saying is it is a real choice.'

A real choice. Really choosing something that might end up being nothing, really choosing to pry yourself open enough to let life in and leaving just enough space for loss, really choosing something expensive, something invasive, something you might need to choose again. What does all that choosing do? What is the cost of not choosing? Or not choosing in time?

Sheree, 33, was determined to stay single for a year when she was 26 and so on a first date, she didn't waste energy trying to be the kind of chill girl we're led to believe men fall in love with. 'I basically said I want kids one day and he said he was the same and then we didn't talk about it again for a long time,' she says.

Sheree just made it to the end of the year as a single woman but by December they were falling in love. They moved in together and three years later she raised the question of having children. He was avoidant, uninterested in the conversation and never indicated that he might have changed his mind. 'He knew I wanted kids and that I thought we would have kids and he never corrected me,' she says.

When Sheree was 30 she went to the doctor about her irregular periods and requested a hormone test to get an idea of her ovarian reserve. The doctor told her to talk to her partner about whether they wanted kids before getting the test so they could face the results together. He never gave her a clear answer, so she never got the test. She came to believe that asking for clarity was asking for too much.

For the next couple of years she put his comfort over her long, unchanging desire to be a mother. Eventually she told him: 'If you've changed your mind you have to tell me definitively because it is a deal breaker and I've spent so much time in this relationship. I obviously love you but this is really important to me.' He asked her for more time to think about it. Months passed, the bushfires raged on, the pandemic came, the city came out of a lockdown and she asked for his answer. 'I haven't really thought about it,' he admitted, a year later. When she broke up with him he was devastated. 'I just told him that I didn't want to wait even though I knew going out on my own the chances of this happening were low. I just knew it wasn't worth it to stay here with this uncertainty,' she says.

Sheree had the test which revealed she likely had a low number of eggs and was told by her doctor to freeze her eggs immediately. During the egg harvesting process she had two failed egg retrievals, as the doctors could not get enough eggs to freeze. They told her she had the egg count of a woman more than a decade older. 'My first reaction was vindication because my instinct about my fertility was right and then came regret that I hadn't done it sooner and then the anger,' she says.

The shapeless, deafening anger that echoed through the socially sanctioned silence about fertility, the indignant rage at her ex for not finding the words while her options were shrinking and then a small, quiet frustration at herself for not trusting her intuition.

The first thing she mourned was the sequence – love, engagement, marriage, children – that she had always assumed she would follow as a child of two culturally traditional parents. But in the space where her expectations had been she found the comforting conviction that motherhood was something she wanted with or without someone else. 'I think I have a lot of value to give as a mother even if it is just me,' she says. 'The option that fills me with the most joy, calms me and feels right is doing it alone and having a donor. It makes so much sense and if it doesn't work out that will be heartbreaking but I can accept that as a reality more than I can hoping and holding out and waiting for someone else.'

One of Sheree's friends mentioned seeing her ex's profile on a dating app shortly after the breakup. 'Wants kids someday,' it read.

'Oh my god are you serious?' I gasp, shedding any pretence of professionalism.

'I know,' she says, laughing.

'Wow. What a luxury to have that time to change your mind so much.'

'Right!'

My mother told me when I came, ten years after her third child, she thought something would go wrong with the pregnancy because she was so old. She was thirty-four. I laughed at the time but now I know that if you conceive after the age of 35 it is referred to as a geriatric pregnancy.

Between 2010 and 2018 the number of egg freezing cycles in Australia and New Zealand increased by 860 per cent. Not every cycle will collect many eggs, not all eggs make embryos, not all embryos result in pregnancies and not all pregnancies will give you a child. The reality is that if I decide I want to have a child in the next few years, I still don't know how stressed I should actually be about whether I could. I call up Kate Stern, a fertility specialist in Melbourne who I have interviewed before, to talk to her about how valid fertility panic is for people in their late 20s. We talk about fertility diminishing with age, the limits of egg freezing, the distinction between the number of eggs and the quality of eggs you have, the fact egg quality actually improves in your early 20s before it declines. We talk about the ungenerous stereotype of the foolish careerist who couldn't hear her biological clock over her noisy ambition and left it too late. Kate says most people seeking IVF just haven't found the right partner to make a family with. 'A few people do egg freezing because they're ambivalent but most people do it because they really want a child,' she says. We talk about the sheer effort required of some patients – Kate has supported trans men who propel themselves into months of body dysmorphia by going off their testosterone to ovulate, collect and freeze their eggs. I wonder if I have ever seriously yearned for anything.

'It's important to be upfront about the changes and the risks and benefits, even when it is hard for our patients to hear,' Kate says. She will tell a patient what their chance of conception was when they first started IVF and then how it has changed. 'So I'll be saying to a 43-year-old woman, "Right now your chance of conceiving is less than 5 per cent and you have a 50 per cent risk of miscarriage. Do you think it is worth it?"' For many people, it is.

Once again I am calling an expert not to hear explanations of her subject matter but to hear how she manages the hope and despair, in this case other people's, involved in making a family. 'You have to know when to call it, when there is no hope left, but we often stop well before that,' Kate says. No hope, in this case, means zero hope, a zero per cent chance of pregnancy. 'You have to be brutally honest and it would be great to be able to say there is a zero chance and that would be easy but by that point often there is like a 5 per cent chance.' Kate describes a patient who had been through two other fertility clinics by the time she reached her and eventually conceived. She reminded Kate afterwards that they had discussed stopping. 'She said, "I have this beautiful baby" and I said, "I know but we had to make sure that you were clear about where you were".' Kate says when she has to call it, she acknowledges that this is when a different kind of grief begins, whether that is considering an egg donor or whether there are no other available options and it is the end of the road. 'One of the most important things we do is helping people finish.'

Finish. For years I have used the word in writing about family planning, to talk about hysterectomies or vasectomies – the ends snipped off, a bow tied around a completed family. *Finished.* But how do you finish wanting? How do you finish trying? Do you only know your exhaustion point once you reach it? What if it stretches far beyond your finances? What if it doesn't match your partner's? What comes after? I am still listening, straining for the sound of a starting gun. If you don't know whether your desire has a beginning, how do you fathom its end?

I began the nine months of searching and writing nervous that I was spending so many words wondering if inside myself there hid something we learn is as unlaboured and spontaneous as conception itself – *'you just know'*. As if parenthood is first sown as an invisible, hermetic desire that precedes an effortless creation, as if the answer comes before any question. But in each interview, I saw an interrogation of self that needed to be so conclusive they could hear the clear, loud pulse of wanting by the end of it. The question was work; the answer was work. I was in awe of how each person braved the friction and the fight, opening themselves up to the vulnerability of creation. I felt my fear in presence of their courage. I no longer felt protected by my ambivalence, reassured I might not ever expose myself to loss. Instead, I noticed that in the time since I first decided to prevent motherhood, my relationship to desire itself had shifted.

Throughout my 20s my desire was incrementally defined in relation, but more often in reaction, to what I found I did not want. I did not want to live in fear. I did not want to live in this or that share house anymore. I did not want to use exercise, drugs, alcohol or attention to avoid discomfort. I did not want to work at a job where men were encouraged to be vile. I did not want to be taken advantage of. I did not want to be defined by low expectations. I did not want unhealthy partnerships or fair-weather friendships. I did not want my friends to suffer. I did not want to play a victim. I did not want to choose dishonesty over discomfort. I did not want to enable anyone. I did not want to let anyone down.

I kept pushing off a wall of experiences I did not want to repeat, propelling myself towards something I had not yet defined. No after no after no . . . I scorched the earth and set a low bar above it. Each year I learn new ways to hold the worst and best in others and in the world. I now understand the value of forgiving, repairing, maintaining. Now I find desire moves through me as hunger not evasion. I am finished building boundaries and find myself opening, wanting something not just for what it isn't but for what it is, for what it could be, a pursuit I once deemed as selfish but now necessary. I saw in these families a desire to create, to say yes again and again and again to something with all its risks and unknowns. I want to say yes, whether to parenthood or something else. I do not want to do that alone.

The protagonist in Sheila Heti's *Motherhood* rejected the identity 'not a mother' because she wanted to protect her sense of self from becoming 'the negative of someone else's positive identity'. But that someone else is always a potential projection of yourself. Fertility forces us to sit with shades of perhaps, maybe, hopefully, hopefully not, overlapping at angles, a misshapen pile of photo negatives, the shadow and light of other lives unlived. On the grey ultrasound, I can see the white limbs of my IUD outstretched like the arms of a clock.

Reflecting and refracting

I couldn't stop calling people. Months before I paused to consider my own perspective, I kept asking, recording, transcribing, reading, note-taking, trying to understand, outstretched towards people who allowed me to hold their stories for long enough to feel the weight of them. I would fall asleep to the sound of their voices, studying the shape of their situations as though it was a Rorschach test through which I could interpret my own. Mothers, fathers, people who knew they would never be parents willingly or unwillingly, people who wanted to tell me about their births, their miscarriages, their parental leave, the way their husbands had learned to clean. I couldn't stop having those first calls, even once I knew there were too many case studies to possibly interview, even once I realised so many of their stories were better suited to a different book, even once I knew it would be impossible to fit them all into nine months. I sent so many emails thanking and apologising, thanking and apologising.

I didn't know how to explain that their stories were important and relevant and so were everybody else's. I was used
to making quick summaries, neat conclusions, publishing
multiple stories a day, tomorrow's fish and chip paper, a link
three pages into a search result. This was not a reporting
assignment and it was not research. It was not empirical.
It was not impersonal. It was a 28-year-old woman calling
strangers, hoping someone would reflect back to her what
she thought she wanted.

My boyfriend's genius brother sends me a philosophy paper. I can't stop laughing. Every sentence makes
a mockery of the way I have gone about answering this
question. The author, Laurie Ann Paul, a Yale professor
of philosophy and cognitive science, argues that normal
models of decision-making theory simply can't be applied
to the decision of whether or not to have a child. Unlike
other choices where we can assume and assign value to
different outcomes based on our preferences, this question
deals with what she calls a 'transformative experience', one
that changes the values and preferences you held before
making the decision.

Paul refers to philosopher Frank Jackson's thought
experiment in which a brilliant neuroscientist Mary is
locked in a colourless cell from birth and while she knows
all the science behind light and the human eye's response
to it, she can't know the colour red until she has experienced
it. 'She experiences redness for the first time, and from this
experience, and this experience alone, she knows what it

is like to see red,' Paul writes. Mary does not know how it will feel to see red but even if she could know that red might fill her heart with joy or fear, she can't know what it is to experience it. She cannot know how she will be forever changed by redness.

And so, from my 'impoverished epistemic position', there is no point imagining the reds I might know – the faint line of a pregnancy test or the last unpicked bloom of period blood seizing a cotton liner as I reach menopause. Until I have experienced having children or experienced never having children, I cannot know what it is like. Asking people with or without children how their lives have changed will tell me little about my own future. You can't assign values to either choice as you don't know how it will transform what you know and how you feel and so you can't determine the relevant outcomes of each act, nor how likely they are. 'The subjective unpredictability attending the act of having one's first child makes the story about family planning into little more than pleasant fiction,' Paul writes.

Does it count for nothing that I have washed, changed, read to, and bargained with a child I would die for? I know the red urgent love that surfaces in specks when a child grazes his knee. Does it count for nothing that I know what it feels like to have no dependents? I know how it feels to circle my lips in rouge self-love and go out whenever and wherever I want only to come home and sleep alone diagonally for as long as I want. Throughout her paper, Paul scrunches up my chapters of dithering, my tens of thousands of words trying to prove that I am an animal of reason, my unearned fear, my unearned hope, the napkin on which I have scrawled pros and cons, and puts them all in the bin. 'I suspect that the popular conception of how to decide to have a child stems from a contemporary ideal of personal psychological development through choice,' she writes. 'That is, a modern conception of self-realization involves the notion that one achieves a kind of maximal self-fulfilment through making reflective, rational choices about the sort of person one wants to be.'

I highlight the sentence and scrawl: *Check her age!! Not a millennial.*

There is something fragile about an identity forged only through personal choices. We collapse our connections to other humans into ourselves, an isolating process of dicing ourselves into smaller pieces that the world as we know it depends on. This individualising, this withdrawal into ourselves, is one of the reasons I first saw motherhood as unattainable for me. The fortification of the nuclear family, the formalisation of so many relationships, a consolidation of the smallest community of three at the expense of participation in a larger one. I wanted to interrogate this question, I wanted to show my working before I had those conversations with my partner and eventually with my friends and family. In writing, in choosing, I felt this instinct to contain my needs within my closest relationships hurdle beyond my loved ones and into my interviews as I strained to hear my own story beneath theirs.

The Most Important Job in the World

My eyes keep getting worse. In the second trimester of writing, I go back to the optometrist for another test and he confirms for the third time in two years that I need stronger lenses. I have six pairs of glasses, all different prescriptions. I tell him about the increasing number of distracting grey squiggles floating across my vision. He asks me how often I look up from my medium-sized screen and not, he insists, just to look at my small-sized screen. I picture myself as I had been for months, a hunched prawn at a desk, switching between screens, transcribing interviews and reading documents and then later relaxing in front of the very big screen at my boyfriend's house. The optometrist tells me to look at the horizon frequently. 'You have to learn to look past the squiggles and into the distance and you will find they don't annoy you so much. They will also disappear when you blink.' I feel unable to look far enough beyond and unable to close my eyes and go deep enough inside myself.

A friend tells me that when she is overwhelmed, she curls up in a foetal position under a blanket and imagines going back in time to just before she had left the womb. 'We know all babies deserve love and they haven't learned to hate themselves yet, and I start from there,' she says. 'When I focus on myself at that stage things don't seem noisy.' One morning I put my quilt over myself and close my eyes. I try to move backwards to a time before I bloomed. Before I opened myself up to the warmth and wind of other people, before I was lavender soothing, chamomile calming, before discolouration and asymmetry jeopardised my worth, before I knew how fragile my parts were, before I knew they could grow back. Outside, my housemates sleep, the planes roar above, the trains scrape past and the lorikeets laugh. I bring my knees up towards my chin, the ridges of my spine flaring, a seashell, listening inside of herself for the sound of the ocean she came from. I mistake sounds for things they're not. Bins dragged to the kerb sound like the early rumblings of a thunderstorm. I am so full. I feel swollen with other people's decisions, my own feelings diluted. I wait until the sounds disappear, until my body is a silent crypt but for my beating heart. Is there anything that so quickly confirms what you love and fear most about the world and yourself, like the question of whether or not to have children? My anxieties about the world rush forward, extraverted, bellowing about the end times. My fears about myself are almost inaudible. I buy a tarot reading in case she can reveal my fate.

I realise no one is going to write the ending for me.

I keep making calls.

The parents make me feel young and untethered. The childfree people recoiling away from parenthood make me realise I am only leaning. Their certainty is moreish. I call Victoria, who loves being an auntie but when she and her husband hold babies, waiting for a sign they should procreate, they feel nothing. Victoria says there is no bodily urge nor rational reason she would ever want children. 'So many of the things that women are expected to do are based in a tradition that no longer belongs here,' she tells me. 'In heterosexual relationships, you get married and you lose your last name, then you have kids and you lost your first name because you just become 'Mum' and you've lost your job in one way or another whether you go back part-time or not at all . . . First name, last name, job, all gone. What's left?' This is how Victoria sees motherhood – loss after loss. It would only jeopardise her personhood, distract from her wonderful relationship and worsen the chronic migraines she lives with. Importantly, it would derail her ambitions as a writer and actor. 'The only thing that I would drive myself through extraordinary pain and trauma for is career-based because that is how much I love it,' she says. 'My identity and what I want to do with my life is to tell stories. It is not just a thing that I do, it is who I am.'

'*Imagine*,' I think later, '*knowing who you are.*'

There is nothing miraculous nor magical about pregnancy. 'I think it is a parasite and I think it would be cumbersome,' she says, my eyes widening as I transcribe. 'I think about how heavy you must feel and how difficult it must be . . . It makes me uncomfortable. It truly does.'

I call Lucy, who tells me her ex-partner was planning on carrying any child they would have together. 'The more I became comfortable in my butch identity, the more the idea of being pregnant and my body changing scared me,' she says. 'I have narrow hips and small breasts and I like that . . . I wonder if I had a more feminine figure if I would

269

have taken steps to alter my body.' Lucy had never felt the urge to have children. 'I've still never felt those ovary pains,' she says. 'I've always felt a bit alien for not feeling it.' But her partner wanted kids and so Lucy figured she would become a parent not out of any compulsion of her own but as a compromise to be with the woman she loved. 'I was delaying making the decision with her and avoiding coming to terms with what the dread and over-whelm eventually meant because I was in a partnership.' It wasn't just pregnancy but motherhood itself that loomed as an unwelcome disruption to her relationship with her body and gender. 'I see my relationship to womanhood as more of a collective, almost political relationship. I relate to the experiences of being oppressed in the patriarchy and of finding camaraderie with other women and within that I include trans women,' she says. 'But I don't have a very personal relationship to womanhood and so being called a woman is kind of okay because it feels like I am part of a collective whereas daughter, sister and mother feel like definitions relating to someone else . . . you're not a person anymore – you're a mother.'

When they broke up Lucy felt relief underneath the sadness. 'Maybe I'm just a selfish prick but I want to be who I want to be and I want to do what I want to do,' she laughs. 'I want to be able to dictate my own life direction and not be so worried that I'm running a small person's life and have someone else dependent on me.' She wants to keep spontaneity, to spend time in her community and have enough energy and time to offer her loved ones and their children – 'and still go home to my own bed'. When Lucy met her current partner she realised they weren't in a rush – to have kids, to get married, to own a home. 'It gave me the space and freedom and relief to not feel like we were on a timed path and to take our time.' They are happy living as they are. 'There is this blankness on the horizon and this freedom to create whatever path we want, in the past it might have terrified me but now I get excited about the idea of it,' she says. 'This temporal freedom.'

Timing, timing, timing. The word punctuated the transcript of my conversation with Melissa.

Seventeen years after her first abortion, she was booked in for another one a month before her 38th birthday. Melissa's first pregnancy was during university. 'I knew that I wasn't supposed to be responsible for another human life and that I could not provide for it or guarantee it or myself the quality of life that we deserved.' In the intervening years she had never imagined herself with or without children but as time went on, she was content with the likelihood she would never be a mother. This time she had written a pros and cons list. Her partner did not want to keep the pregnancy so together they decided to make an appointment. The clinic assured her she could cancel at any time. Melissa found herself sobbing in the shower. 'I just broke down and I thought, "*I cannot terminate this pregnancy*".' Their baby was born a few months before we speak.

It wasn't a realisation that she had wanted to be a mother all along, it was a realisation that she had arrived at a position in her life where motherhood was right for her. Her partner took to fatherhood instantly and excitedly, and Melissa found herself coping with motherhood better than she had predicted. 'One of the reasons why motherhood is a thing I feel confident in now is because I am in an emotional and financial position to provide for a family,' she says. 'Everything I had thought about timing was valid.'

I go and get a facial, and by that I mean I try to purchase the confidence I need to finish the nine months of writing because internal metrics of self-worth only apply to women you care about more than you do yourself. The beautician solemnly tells me I am ageing prematurely and I buy the expensive cream she recommends because her skin is gleaming like a freshly peeled lychee. On the bus home I see myself, suddenly a crone, in the reflection. I search for egg-freezing clinics near me.

For nine months, time hunts me like this, in bursts. Sometimes, I don't feel chased. I feel safely transported by the seasons, along tracks I cannot see. Time does not hand me my coat, press a guiding palm to the small of my back and usher me out towards a decision like I'd hoped it might. Instead time allows me to write, and through the words I feel myself changing.

I find, as Deborah Levy did, not only that the idea of the mother 'as imagined and politicised by the societal system, was a delusion', but that my own ideas of her did not stand up to scrutiny. A person from a family that is now only ever in the same room at a funeral did not know how to create something close, loving and stable. A person who could not cleanly resolve her angst about the future was not fit to deliver a child into the murk of it. A person who did not inherently know she was a mother could never become one.

I began reimagining motherhood and not-motherhood. I needed time to sit with the flaws in the feminism I knew best. This feminism wanted more choice and more freedom but it could also be fast, anti-maternal, power-hungry, self-interested, isolating, a handmaiden to capitalism. It does not value what I do – care, maintenance, community, inclusivity, forgiveness. I needed to admit that regardless of my choice, I value motherhood and do not want to participate in its degradation anymore. I do not want to buy into a binary in which mothers are not as savvy, creative, intellectual, ambitious or interesting, just as I know they are not more selfless or caring than women without children. I realised I want my decision to be made with the full knowledge that motherhood was not the only way to love deeply and fulfil someone else's needs and that life without children was not the only way to connect to yourself and your own potential. I want a life without my own children that is still rooted in connectivity, that is still in service of others, that still involves other people's children. I want a motherhood expansive enough to incorporate personhood, to embrace humanity. A person who makes mistakes and is not crucified for them, a person who has her own needs, a person who just wants to be a mother more days than she does not.

Every week I see updates on social media from a friend of my brother's, who he met in rehab. Her two sons were taken away from her because the family was experiencing violence and she was in addiction. The last time I saw her in person she was still trying to get full custody of her boys and needed to prove she was dry and clean. In this limbo she was recommitting to motherhood, reimagining herself as a mother again. As a good mother, she told me. She said she would spend her life making it up to them, earning their trust and keeping them safe. They are now reunited and I see them thriving, each football game and birthday a miracle she celebrates. She reminds me that being a parent is not something you choose just once. In my efforts not to romanticise motherhood I had spent too much time wondering how people had the strength to survive it and forgetting how it could help you to find the strength to survive.

'It's true what they say, that a baby gives you a reason to live,' Rivka Galchen wrote. 'But also, a baby is a reason that it is not permissible to die. There are days when this does not feel good.' When I began writing I saw parenthood only as permanence, an immutable relationship to another human, a shackling to the world as it is and to yourself as you are. I had decided the people around me who were choosing to have kids had reached a heroic self-possession and a peace with the future that I was incapable of. I am not sure that is right anymore. I am redefining bravery.

The question of whether or not to have a child became an exercise in tracking my fear about the world and extending it beyond my own lifespan. Civilisation is collapsing and humanity has been rendered infertile by 2027 in the film *Children of Men*. 'Fugees' flee to a militarised Britain, where they are hunted down and jailed. Humans are on the brink of extinction until Kee, a fugee, falls pregnant, a miracle the world has been waiting for. The film follows her struggle to safely reach a secret scientific group so she can be studied to cure the two decades of global infertility. As Gavin Jacobson writes, the future of humanity has been placed in the body of 'perhaps the most powerless, disenfranchised, stigmatised and exploited individual in the modern Great Chain of Being' – a Black refugee woman. 'Kee is the antithesis of almost everything that modern societies venerate and forgive: the rich, the male, the rooted, the documented,' Jacobson writes. 'She is the film's true apocalypse in the literal sense of the word – pure revelation, forcing us to confront the hollowness and turpitude of the prevailing moral order.' I thought the film would be useful to watch, to add to my growing appendix of texts in which children are synonymous with hope and so without them despair flourishes and chaos ensues. Instead I was struck by how real this world felt. As philosopher Slavoj Žižek writes, this is not an alternate reality; the directors have instead 'simply [made] reality more what it already is'. I do not want to be a person who, with all her privilege, with all her resources, can more easily conceptualise collapse than change. Imagining the end of procreation should not be easier than imagining a world in which we can transform the forces that make creating new life so fraught. I ask what I want from my life and how do I want to live through the horror of a virus that has only laid bare what was already there. The pandemic shatters each community differently but we fracture along lines that were already drawn.

A pollster tweeted a graph that showed that in the four years to August 2021 an increasing number of Americans believed this statement was very or somewhat likely: 'Given the events you have witnessed over your life-time, how likely do you think it is that we are currently living in a version of a negative afterlife (e.g. hell, purgatory, or a similar concept)?' When interviewed by journalist Luke O'Neil, the author Casey Taylor said the question began as a joke 'at the peak of mass hysteria' when US president Donald Trump was elected but when it became clear one in three people thought it was feasible they lived in hell he looked more closely at the data.

'When I dove into the crosstabs, it started to become clear that "hell" acted as a proxy for cyclical, institutional problems in America,' he told O'Neil. 'Women and people of colour were more likely to believe it was possible.

Lower classes and the unemployed. People with debt, or medical problems they can't solve.'

I want my doom to be instructive, not conclusive.

When writer Jia Tolentino was interviewed while eight months pregnant in mid-2020, she said there isn't an 'ethical justification for having kids' at a time when existing human suffering and racial and economic inequities were only escalating, especially during a pandemic. 'But I am committed to the idea that the world can be better,' she said. 'And I have some amount of faith that being human, being able to love, is still an untouchably and unpredictably generative thing – worthwhile across unknown contexts, in and of itself.' Is there a more staggering display of hope than to bring new life into a world you believe is unstable and dangerous? It looks like hope as Rebecca Solnit defines it; not as a 'lottery ticket' that you hold feeling lucky but 'an axe you break down doors with in an emergency'.

Each week, I ask in different ways: is it fair to force children to sharpen themselves in a world we have made so abrasive? Each week I feel challenged to learn how to hope more usefully. I felt frustrated with myself that I had not already managed to do this as a person without children.

While waiting for the arrival of his son into a world he deemed mostly 'bad', Tom Whyman identified three main qualities as antithetical to hope. I harboured them all. He identifies cynicism – calming our fear of our own desire for a better world by branding that desire as stupid, dangerous and delusional; from resignation – deciding we have no power to work towards a better world; and despair – the absence of any belief in a better world. He makes a case for cultivating more hopeful virtues; charity – a 'do-gooding' for others that Whyman defines as an intellectual value rather than a blanketing moral one; solidarity – acting for the collective interest; and finally modesty – a knowledge that progress isn't absolute and an awareness of what we can achieve alone and together. 'To be truly hopeful, we must be able to recognise some good which transcends our own discrete self-interest – and being invested in the interests of future generations, in whatever capacity whether it be as a parent or a grandparent or a godparent or an aunt or an uncle or a teacher or a campaigner or an artist or a friend – is one (perhaps the most readily available) direct, practical way we have of realising this transcendent good *immanently* in the world.' I want to hope better. The choice to try to do so is the simplest part.

I call Whyman to find out whether his hope had changed shape since becoming a father. He tells me parenthood has confirmed for him the wisdom of two of Nietzsche's concepts. The first is that of 'eternal recurrence' – the idea that everything in the world perpetually repeats itself in cycles. In Nietzsche's thought experiment – I don't possess the intellect to engage with it as an actual metaphysical theory – he tells the reader to imagine a demon who comes to them at their 'loneliest loneliness' and asks them to imagine reliving their life as they have lived it with every pain and every joy.

'I used to think that was just monstrous,' Whyman tells me, and I find myself agreeing. In the throes of decision-making the idea adds an unbearable, if hypothetical, weight – would I choose having kids again? Would I choose never having kids again?

'But now I realise if I'd done anything in my life different prior to his conception [my son] wouldn't have existed,' Whyman says. 'I can see why I would want everything in the universe to be the same up until now because it means he is here.'

This is the second idea of Nietzsche's that fatherhood has fortified for Whyman, that of *amor fati* or love of fate – an active embrace of all that has happened in life as necessary.

I discover the philosopher Laurie Ann Paul is fifty-four. She speaks with the considered cadence of an NPR host. She paces across a stage, her hands gesticulating, adding confident exclamation marks to her words. She would never spend the time it takes to grow a baby dithering on the page about whether or not she should. She would never conceive of herself as a rational agent. Paul says she does not believe it is right or wrong to have children, nor that people shouldn't be happy with their decision. 'My view is simply that you need to be honest with yourself about the basis for this choice.'

John J Kaag believes Nietzsche was not asking people to obsess over the rightness or wrongness of their decisions but to liberate themselves by taking responsibility for them. 'Perhaps the hardest part of the eternal return is to own up to the tortures that we create for ourselves and those we create for others,' Kaag writes. 'Owning up: to recollect, to regret, to be responsible, ultimately to forgive and love.'

For years I did not know how to describe a particular sensation that sometimes overcame me without someone thinking it was suicidal ideation or a fantasy of self-harm. I knew it was neither but it looks bad on paper and so on paper was where I left it. If you were to trace a line north from your navel along your torso and pause at the last place that it is soft, just before the hard bracket of your sternum, right there, that is the spot. Every so often I would feel a strong and sudden desire to pierce it with a knife. It happened in times of self-doubt or guilt, especially if I thought I had inconvenienced, offended or hurt someone but I knew it was not an urge to mutilate my body. My flesh just happened to be in the way of this rock of a feeling I wanted to shuck and drain. I could almost feel the blood rushing towards my centre looking not for violence but for deliverance – for peace.

The psychologist I was seeing in my early 20s took out a piece of paper and drew a line travelling gradually up the page from the bottom left to top right corner. This was not how self-reflection and healing worked, he told me. It was not a satisfying upward linear trajectory towards enlightenment and freedom. Then he drew another line but this time it looped around and around before reaching the top of the page. Growth was a long slow trudge in a circle on a slight incline. Again and again you would have to face your darkest parts. They might get less shadowy on approach but they would still be there on the next lap. There was no summit. He offered me the piece of paper, blank but for the spiral and the straight line. 'It's okay,' I said. 'I think I can remember that.'

I thought I knew what I would tour past. I was yet to learn that you can see and experience things that loved ones or lawmakers deem hard and still flourish. Nothing ever feels as it looks on paper.

The pen circled around and around my mother. I felt a horrified guilt when I thought of the C-section scar left by my birth. I was told I was an afterthought rather than an accident but I felt like an albatross.

I have always felt my mother's emotions as mine. We have spent more time alone together than anyone else in the family because I was born a decade after my parents' third child and my parents separated when I was still a toddler. I have always felt we are irreconcilably different yet made of the same stuff. I am protective of her at her second wedding, after a decade of the two of us living on and off together alone, I felt like I was the one giving her away. In my sessions I looped past her emotional needs and my incapacity to meet them or to establish boundaries so that

I wouldn't feel the need to once I'd left home. I feared that I was not the daughter she wanted; a daughter with similar values who had an interest in establishing a family. It took a while to get to the truth of why I felt like this. I told the psychologist in snippets of a series of memories in which, in the chaos of our family, my mother had withdrawn love, whether in stress or frustration or fear or exhaustion. They were not the nights we ended up sleeping somewhere else; they were flashes of anger and absence I knew she rarely, if ever, thought of now. She might not remember them because she had already seen too much of life and had four children. I would never forget them because I had not seen enough of life and had one mother. These moments, hard beads on a string marking the timeline of my life so far, felt unbearable to think about. I found myself unable to speak so he asked me if I could feel where in my body I was experiencing the pain of the memories. My hand moved instinctively to my chest and then down to the spot. I rested my hand there and cried silently. He told me there would be no confrontation. He said this was on-her-deathbed stuff. To make peace with it, we would revisit these moments again and again. I stopped seeing him soon after. I did not want to slowly slice myself open.

I always thought a pearl began to form when a grain of sand entered an oyster but it is usually a tiny invading organism. 'Then, something miraculous happens,' the *National Geographic* voice over tells me. The mollusc responds to the intruder by secreting a smooth crystalline substance called

282

nacre, or mother-of-pearl. 'It takes several years for thousands of layers of nacre to build up and create a smooth iridescent gem but it's a rare event,' he says. 'A pearl of value is found in less than one in 10,000 wild pearl oysters.' As MFK Fisher wrote, 'the unwelcome worm is encased in its rare coffin', coated in a protective material.

Nacre is stronger and lighter than concrete. Scientists tried to work out how a random process in which different cells simultaneously secreted materials around the mollusc could result in such exemplary engineering. Faults replicated through layers 'like a helix' but somehow the material ended up sturdy and uniformly structured, Dr Igor Zlotnikov said in an interview. 'How could perfection emerge from such disorder?' he marvelled. The scientists discovered that defects from opposite ends of the mollusc moved towards each other until they met and synchronised. The material toughened as it was stressed.

I had long accepted that my relationship with my mother would be imperfect. I had accepted there would still be joy to be found in the future and in the past. I had accepted her not just as a mother, not just as a woman but as a human being who, like most humans, is doing so much more than expected. I found a new gratitude for all the gifts she had given me. Her joy. The endless and infectious enthusiasm for life which turned errands into adventures. I can see her dancing down supermarket aisles, chucking discounted chocolates into the trolley, testing my teenage sullenness until I joined her. Her commitment to humour.

Her acute allergy to anything affected, snobbish or, in her words, 'indulgent'. Her unshakable loyalty. Her fearlessness in the face of other people's pain. The turning up, turning up, turning up. Her connection to her own pleasure and her steadfastness in pursuing it. An afternoon at the beach reading a crime novel, a bag of dresses on sale hauled home from an outlet, a freshly baked lamington bursting with cream. Her ability to multitask which I can only remember failing her once when we T-boned a P-plater who had swerved into our path while driving through a country town. It happened right in front of a police officer stationed with a speed camera, as if we were all trying to give him extra work. Mum had been smoking a cigarette out the window, singing along to the radio, peeling a mandarin, sipping a Diet Coke and almost instantly answering the cryptic cross-word clues I was reading out. She told the police officer it was his fault as he had distracted her, and he laughed. We bought new swimming costumes at Target and waited at a motel for the car to be repaired. Another adventure. '*Thank you, thank you, thank you,*' I say when I feel my attention draining down my breastbone towards my belly.

Molluscs improve the quality of the water around them by removing excess nitrogen and incorporating it into their bodies as they grow. Fake pearls will stay cool and smooth but a real pearl will warm with your skin and feel gritty if you run it along your teeth. I watch video after video of people wrenching open different oysters, mussels and clams. They fumble around in the protective tissue, a complex filtration system that lives between the pearl and the mother of the pearl, and wrench out the gleaming gem, an unannounced visitor made precious from the organism's flesh and bone.

I will never understand why I decided to email her two trimesters in to the nine months. I have tried to retrace my steps but it just happened. It had taken years to accept we would never have the very conversation it took me less than an hour to start. I breached the terms and conditions she had set for our relationship and then waited for my proof that maternal love was conditional. I hit send and went for a walk. I watched the sun set knowing I might have risked her withdrawing love indefinitely.

I told her how much I loved her. I acknowledged how much good and bad we had been through together. I explained how hard it was to write a book in which I was repeatedly expressing opinions she herself did not hold. I knew what she saw as political or ideological differences were not just a contest of ideas for me but a constant reminder that I was unable to value what she did. To write this book, to write this email, was to make someone uncomfortable, to take up space, to have needs, to be visible. It was to risk love.

I did not tell her about the knife but I tried to draw the outline of what it was trying to spear. I said that I was content to deceive my readers of my book, then half written, but I could not deceive her of a realisation I'd had soon after I gave myself this deadline. Underneath the fear about the smoke in the air, the gender inequity, the precarious work-force, down past the colourless coral in the depths of myself was my relationship with her, unopened. I feared that even if I found myself wanting a child, there was a deeper and dormant *not* wanting that would only emerge once I had a child. In order to know I was capable of wanting, I wanted to know she had wanted me. I apologised that the years of care, love and tenderness could not eclipse a handful of moments I felt were confirmations of my unwantedness.

My mother replied at first with a text, asking for a day to respond but assuring me that I was loved and that love was unconditional. In the email there was no defensiveness, no denial, no avoidance. It was just my mother, the clearest I have ever and will ever see her.

'I have never felt anything but love for you.' She described what motherhood feels like. I had never asked. She told me about the beauty, the terror, the singular intensity. I instantly remembered her telling me once she had slept with one hand in the cot to make sure my chest was rising and falling. I understood that parenting is mostly holding fear for someone you love. She wrote that I was the child with whom she finally had the time, space and financial security to appreciate the wonder of me 'growing, changing and responding'. We emailed back and forth, both of us crying. Salt water on my keyboard. This was what it felt like to finally believe something you wanted to be true.

When I saw her in person we did not speak of it but something had changed. We were not attacking and we were not defensive. Nayyirah Waheed wrote that some people contract and others expand when you tell them your story, and that is 'how you know'. My mother allowed herself to split open, as she had when I was cut from an incision in her abdomen, so we could see how we were together and apart from each other, our past and present illuminated. My grit within her, hers within me.

Elena Ferrante has written that when it comes to mothers, reconciliation does not involve forgetting wrongs but seeing our mother as we did when we were children. 'I was reconciled with mine when I felt those wrongs – what seemed to me wrongs – as part of myself, essential for my development. So essential that they now appear an invention of mine, a brightly coloured exaggeration.'

Mother-of-pearl appears iridescent because its comprising platelets of aragonite are so thin they are close to the wavelength of visible light. Fake pearls will shine but real pearls will glow, the light trapped in miniscule layers of nacre. The surface changes colour because the light is not just reflecting but refracting. I felt briefly whole, nothing needing to be excised. I could feel my blood, warm and red, moving through every part of my body.

In the ninth month, I am completely invested in the health and safety of two uteruses – those of my closest friends. One is in her first trimester of pregnancy. The other is waiting to find out whether the growth pushing into her endometrium is an unusual fibroid or an aggressive cancer. A few weeks before turning 30 she is wondering whether she will need a hysterectomy. A court makes a landmark ruling in favour of climate activists and against Shell, ordering the fossil fuel giant to cut its carbon dioxide emissions and noting the company's activities constituted a threat to the 'right to life'. I begin spontaneously bleeding, waking in the middle of the night with cramps I haven't felt in years. I vomit from the pain. I wonder whether endometriosis is winning the war against my implant.

The elderly lady I read to dies alone. She once told me her late sister visited on her loneliest nights, lying down next to her bed to keep her company but for two years I was her only terrestrial visitor, lockdown restrictions stopping me in the month before her death. She didn't have children because something was wrong with her ovaries, but I can't catch what, even at her most lucid when she describes her beloved cattle dogs and the never-ending blonde fields she grew up on. The residents with children are rarely visited so I will never know if motherhood would have spared her finishing her 103 years on Earth alone in a ward where pigeons roam the corridors.

I go to the pub with a former colleague, her two-year-old and her husband, whose eyes widen excitedly as he tells us that having a child has renewed his sense of wonder in the world. Their daughter hands me pencils, listing each colour. She points at the traffic excitedly. She dips her chips in sauce as though she has never tasted it before. Her name is, of course, literally, Hope. I know if this was a script it would be reworked to prevent scathing reviews from critics about the ham-fisted symbolism invading my life just at the denouement.

It is stories that pulled me into this question and it is stories that are helping me to answer it. Those that we tell about ourselves and about each other. The myths that live on inside us. The chronicles of everyone I called. They self-selected to be interviewed because they understood that their lives had meaning beyond themselves. They wanted to shake and calm, bruise and heal others. The tales of the end of the world. The grand theories of who owns a body. The chapter my partner wants to write next. The editing of what a mother is, who my mother is. The redrafting of what a daughter is, who I am. The story of how I would grow old without a child. The story of who I would be with a child.

The narrativising has transformed me. It is through these stories that I feel the small heel of something true pushing outwards from within me, testing the strength of the limb to which it is attached.

Acknowledgements

Thank you to my agent Rach Crawford for your remarkable talent and the confidence and assistance you gave me to pitch and deliver this book.

Thank you to my editor Cate Blake for completely backing this book and helping me to find my voice.

Thank you to Casey Willoughby for knowing me, yourself, and how humans work better than anyone else and for being family to me.

Thank you to Léa Antigny and Rebecca Slater for opening up your gigantic brains and enormous hearts to me always but especially on Thursdays.

Thank you to Hannah Ryan for helping me to tell the truth in so many ways and for your intuitive brilliance and unstoppable hype.

Thank you to Gyan Yankovich for *always* showing up and bringing cleverness and enthusiasm with you.

Thank you to my mentor Sarah Krasnostein for your wisdom, eerily perceptive psychoanalysis and for somehow producing the best nonfiction in the country without developing a big ego.

Thank you to Aden Knaap, Ruby Munsie, Alex McClintock, Freya Newman, Tahlia Pritchard, Alex Christie, Humyara Mahbub and Laura Southern from Wolf Literary for your generosity in reading bad chapters and helping to make them better ones.

Thank you to the people along the way who made me feel like I could write a book in various encouraging moments probably without even realising it: James Colley, Bec Shaw, Tiger Webb, Alice Mitzi Quinn, Mia Langguth, Lane Sainty, Jess Smith, Alissa Tan and Libby Reid.

Thank you to Chrissie Kerr for making sure those bluebells bloom each spring and celebrating them when they do.

Thank you to Catherine Sinclair for your compassionate and gentle instruction in feeling and not only thinking my way out.

Thank you to Marni Cordell for letting me report on everything I have and for all of your initial advice about this book but most of all for redefining womanhood, and in turn motherhood, for me.

Thank you to all of the people I interviewed for this book and as a journalist. You are all a part of this story even if you are not directly quoted. Thank you to everyone in the reproductive healthcare and rights space who has supported my journalism vocally and protectively from the very beginning.

Thank you to all the thinkers who gave me permission to share their work in this book and those who generously endorsed it.

Thank you to my family. Thank you to my mother, to whom this book is dedicated, for your love, for your labour and for trusting me to write this with care. Thank you to my sister Bridie for letting me grow up within your loving protectiveness and for creating two lucky humans who will experience the same. Thank you to Gabriel Leo for kicking the Sherrin better than any kid in the country! Thank you to Sylvia Josephine for being so clever and such an amazing singer. Thank you to my dad and Lee for nurturing my love of reading and writing. Thank you to my brother Tom for your love.

Thank you to the Stewarts for the time I spent down south where I could write away from my beautiful but bellowing housemates. Thank you to my housemates for trying your best to be quiet.

Finally, thank you to Tim for allowing me to have this conversation with myself before I knew how to have it with you. I love you very much.